HONOR J. CAMPBELL

The Foodwatch Cookbook

Ashgrove Press, Bath

First Published in Great Britain by
ASHGROVE PRESS
Bath Road, Norton St. Philip,
Bath BA3 6LW

© Honor J. Campbell, 1988, 1990, 1992, 1998

ISBN 1-85398-119-2

First published 1988
(as *The Foodwatch Alternative Cookbook*)

New edition 1990
Reprinted 1990
Third edition 1992
Reprinted 1995
Fourth edition 1998

Printed and bound in Great Britain by
Redwood Books
Trowbridge, Wiltshire

Contents

About the Book

My first *Foodwatch Cookbook* was written primarily to show how to make good use of alternative flours. This was followed by second and third enlarged editions, both following this theme. This latest edition contains over 70 new recipes, most of them sugar-free and reflecting the current trend in tastes, plus a whole host of modifications and updates. All the recipes are free of wheat, cows' milk and chemical additives and all are vegetarian. Many of them also incorporate information on using alternative ingredients to give as many variations as possible. A special feature of this edition is the inclusion before each recipe of symbols, known as 'tiles', for four diets: Candida albicans control, egg-free, gluten-free, and grain-free. These 'tiles' make it easy to see at a glance which recipes are suitable for these four diets.

We are fortunate nowadays to have available a wide variety of protein sources, vegetables and fruits all the year round; if you are on a special diet, or catering for someone else who is, main meals are not such a problem as are breakfasts, teatimes and snacks, where many of the foods that are usually eaten are based on wheat or cows' milk. For this reason I have continued in this latest edition to show how alternative cereals and carbohydrates (and there are a surprising number of them) can be used in appetising and nutritious ways that are acceptable to all the family. I feel that it is important that anyone on a special diet is not made to feel ostracised at the meal table; this is especially so where children are concerned.

Good nutrition is vital for all of us, but especially for those on a restricted diet. Be adventurous; try new tastes, don't just stick to what you know, as this can lead to vitamin and mineral deficiencies. Learn which of the foods that you *can* have may be substituted for those you *can't* have. By doing this you can adapt your favourite recipes to suit current needs.

And finally, I hope you enjoy experimenting.

Honor J. Campbell

About the Four Diets

At the beginning of each recipe appears a block of four 'tiles' indicating four diets, like this:

C stands for Candida albicans Control Diet, E for Egg-free Diet, Gl for Gluten-free Diet and Gr for Grain-free Diet. Each recipe is suitable for the diet or diets indicated by the 'tiles'. If a recipe is not suitable for a particular diet, the relevant 'tile' is blank: ☐. Any special instructions relating to a particular diet appear at the end of the recipe and are marked by the relevant 'tile'.

Candida albicans Control Diet

At first this diet is very strict indeed. Foods excluded are: sugar (sucrose), honey, fructose, glucose, malt extract, maple syrup, oat syrup, rice syrup, black treacle, molasses, date syrup, all dried and fresh fruit, mushrooms, yeast, yeast extract, vinegars, tamari (wheat-free soy sauce), refined flours and starches. Yoghurt may have to be excluded, but only if the medical treatment being given warrants it. Some practitioners recommend the exclusion of lactose during the early stages of treatment. Goats' and sheep's milk which contain lactose have been included in these recipes; however soya milk is an acceptable substitute. After a few weeks on the treatment, the diet can be gradually expanded, usually starting with lemon, and notes to this effect appear at the end of certain recipes. The new sugar-free puddings in this edition are not suitable for a Candida albicans Control Diet (except for Sugar-free Carob Puddings). The others come in useful during the transition period before going back to a normal diet. These recipes could become firm favourites, especially Sticky Date Puddings! Extra virgin olive oil is beneficial in the fight against Candida albicans and should, therefore, be used instead of margarine or other oils wherever possible. It is inadvisable to follow this diet without medical supervision, as careful supplementation is needed to avoid or rectify deficiencies of essential minerals and vitamins.

Egg-free Diet

Excluding only one food from the diet sounds simple enough, but eggs are used for so many things, making an egg-free diet quite restrictive without the use of egg replacers. The three Cirrus egg replacers are used to achieve the basic applications of eggs – binding and aeration. The recipes indicated include those where no egg is required at all or in which an egg replacer is used to obtain the required results.

Gluten-free Diet

Gluten is a constituent of wheat, rye, barley and oats, and these four grains along with foodstuffs derived from them should be excluded from the diet. When eating out it is safest to stick to rice or potato, but at home there is a wide range of foods that can be used. The following carbohydrates are available as whole grains, flours, flakes, seeds or pasta and are suitable for a gluten-free diet: maize (corn), millet, rice, buckwheat, amaranth, chick pea, banana, chestnut, potato, sweet potato, yam, sorghum, sago, tapioca, quinoa, lentil, water chestnut, Jerusalem artichoke, soya and arrowroot. The recipes show not only how gluten-free flours and flakes etc. can be made into breads, cakes and puddings but also how main course dishes can be made using many of these gluten-free ingredients.

Grain-free Diet

'Grain-free' excludes from the diet all members of the Graminae family of foods (see page 199). All other flours, flakes, seeds and starches may be used. It is tempting on a grain-free diet to stick to potatoes and when eating out this can be the safest thing to do. However, when at home use as wide a variety of foods as possible and follow the advice above – be adventurous and try new flavours. The following are suitable for a grain-free diet: buckwheat (flour, flakes and groats), amaranth (flour, seeds and flakes), chick pea (gram) flour, banana flour, chestnut flour, quinoa, potato flour, sago flour, tapioca flour, lentil flour, water chestnut flour, soya flour, Jerusalem artichoke flour and arrowroot. There are also 100% Soba (buckwheat noodles), buckwheat pasta spirals and lentil pasta shells, as well as potatoes, sweet potatoes and yams. These recipes show how many of these ingredients can be used to make appetising meals suitable for a grain-free diet.

About the Ingredients

Rye

RYE FLOUR is used in Russia and Europe for breadmaking, the most widely known being Pumpernickel. The flour is dark and low in gluten, making a rather heavy, close-textured bread that has a good flavour and keeps well.

RYE FLAKES are coarse and not suitable for making muesli but can be used for puddings.

Barley

BARLEY FLOUR also contains gluten; it produces a light, crumbly textured loaf with a paler colour than rye. It has been eaten by mankind since early times and, indeed, it was three barley loaves that Jesus used when he miraculously fed the five thousand. The flour is also good for making cakes, biscuits and sponge puddings.

BARLEY FLAKES have a nutty flavour and are used in puddings, parkin and as a quick alternative to pot barley in soups, casseroles and for making barley water.

POT BARLEY is pearl barley with the outer layer left intact and so it takes a lot longer to cook than pearl barley. Nutritionally, though, it is far superior.

Oats

Oats are widely used in manufactured goods and are therefore more familiar to most people than the above two grains. It is the last of the grains in this list to contain gluten.

OATMEAL comes in three grades, fine, medium and coarse, all of which are used for porridge, parkin and oatcakes; which to use is a matter of choice.

PORRIDGE OATS or oat flakes are used for quick porridge, muesli, biscuits, flapjacks, crumble toppings for cakes and puddings, savoury dishes and for making sweets or fruit bars.

OAT BRAN AND OAT GERM are extremely nutritious and can be used as a cereal or as a topping.

Maize (Corn)

Maize has been grown as a food crop for humans for thousands of years.

MAIZEMEAL comes in a number of grades; fine maizemeal is used for making Italian Polenta and coarse is ideal for bread. Muffins can be made from any grade of maizemeal, whichever is to hand.

CORNFLOUR is used to thicken gravies, sauces, blancmanges and custards, as well as in stir-fries and marinades.

POPCORN is a special variety of corn with a hard outer coat and is an easily-made snack or breakfast cereal.

SWEETCORN or CORN ON THE COB is a familiar vegetable, which has a high sugar content. This is a different variety which has been bred for its large succulent, soft-coated grains.

CORN PASTA SPIRALS and CORN SPAGHETTI – see below under Pasta.

Millet

Millet is one of the most nutritious of all the grains and is invaluable for a gluten-free diet.

MILLET FLAKES are used extensively throughout this book because they are so useful; keep them in the storecupboard at all times. They can be used for porridge, biscuits, flapjack, crumble toppings for cakes and puddings, in numerous savoury dishes and in the making of sweets and fruit bars.

MILLET FLOUR is difficult to obtain but can be made in a blender from millet flakes. Use it to make breads and cakes.

MILLET SEED or WHOLE MILLET makes a good substitute for rice and cous cous. As well as being used as an accompaniment it is also used for stuffings for roast vegetables, pilaffs and timbales.

MILLET AND RICE PASTA has to be cooked carefully to retain a good texture. However, it has the advantage of being bland and so it will not detract from the flavours of the other ingredients with which it is served.

Rice

Rice is the staple food for a large percentage of the earth's population, white rice being the most widely used. Popularity, however, does not make it the most nutritious. In fact white rice is nutritionally very poor, as the vitamins and minerals are in the outer coat which has been removed to make the rice white. For someone on a gluten-free diet rice is a very important food and so for maximum nutrition it makes sense to use brown rice.

LONG-GRAIN BROWN RICE takes longer to cook than white rice; it has a nutty flavour and a slightly chewy texture, making it a satisfying accompaniment to any meal.

BROWN RICE FLOUR (100% RICE FLOUR) is the mainstay of gluten-free baking; use it to make waffles, pancakes, biscuits, cakes and sponge puddings. However, for breadmaking it is best mixed with one of the other flours, as is seen from the recipes.

RED RICE originates from the Camargue area of France where it was discovered by the Griotto family who market it: a really full-bodied rice with a delicious flavour and a chewy texture. It is used in the same ways as long-grain brown rice and makes an outstanding addition to a meal.

WILD RICE is an aquatic grass and not really a rice at all, although it is used just like rice. The long dark grains are very slim and have quite a strong flavour. This is why wild rice is often served mixed with white or brown rice.

Buckwheat

Although the name might suggest otherwise, buckwheat is grain-free, being a seed in the same food family as rhubarb.

BUCKWHEAT FLOUR is very dark in colour and has a distinctive flavour which some find a little hard to get used to. However, it may be mixed with potato flour or one of the other starches to produce breads, biscuits and cakes.

BUCKWHEAT FLAKES have a more mellow flavour than the flour because the outer husks have been removed, and are good for cereals, cakes, biscuits, puddings, toppings for cakes and in savoury dishes and sweets.

BUCKWHEAT GROATS are whole buckwheat seeds and can be purchased natural or roasted; they are used mainly in savoury dishes or as an accompaniment instead of rice or millet.

Chestnut

CHESTNUT FLOUR is an unusual flour which makes a useful addition to grain-free breads and savoury biscuits. When it is used in conjunction with potato flour it imparts a very pleasant flavour to the bread, but on its own it is a bit too powerful for most tastes. WHOLE CHESTNUTS are used in savoury dishes and pies. They may be purchased fresh when in season or vacuum-packed for minimal preparation and for when the fresh ones are not available.

Amaranth

AMARANTH is an ancient foodstuff grown by the Aztecs. It is a very nutritious seed which is sold as AMARANTH TOASTED FLOUR, AMARANTH CRUNCHY FLAKES or WHOLE AMARANTH SEEDS. The flour is used along with potato flour to produce grain-free bread and on its own to make savoury biscuits. The flakes are used as a cereal and the seeds, which are very small and hard, are best ground in a coffee grinder to produce an untoasted flour where this is preferred. All three products are available by mail order (see page 19).

Other Grain-free Flours

CHICK PEA FLOUR (GRAM FLOUR) is a useful grain-free flour which is widely available and is used for breads and cakes. It also makes a good savoury batter for fritters (see page 161). Also look out for Puppodums made with gram flour which are also widely available and can be used as a quick substitute for bread at any time as well as being eaten as a traditional accompaniment to curry.

BANANA FLOUR is an unusual grain-free flour; it is produced from a particular variety of bananas which are harvested when still underripe. It has a bland flavour and is particularly useful for making cakes and sponge puddings as it gives a good texture and has a pale colour.

POTATO FLOUR (POTATO FARINA) is actually a starch rather than a flour. It is an important ingredient in grain-free breads, especially as it makes for a lighter texture, and is often mixed with other grain-free flours which add flavour and are more nutritious. It is also used to thicken gravy.

ARROWROOT is the grain-free equivalent of cornflour. It is used to thicken gravy and sauces, to make blancmange, custard and desserts, as well as being used in stir-fries and marinades.

SAGO FLOUR and TAPIOCA FLOUR are both starches which can

be used to make biscuits and shortbread as well as being thickeners.

Raising Agents

GLUTEN-FREE BAKING POWDER. There are a number on the market, most of them containing potato flour, making them suitable for a grain-free diet as well as a gluten-free one. It is this type which has been used in these recipes.

'ARISE' is a raising agent suitable for use in yeast-free breads. It gives a yeast-raised texture to a loaf, and works best with flours containing gluten. Carbon dioxide is generated gradually during baking, instead of very rapidly as with baking powder; this is why the latter produces loaves of a fairly dense texture. 'Arise' needs sodium bicarbonate or potassium bicarbonate to make it effective. A blend of two parts sodium bicarbonate to one part potassium bicarbonate is the most beneficial for health.

'Arise' is available only by mail order (see page 19).

Pasta

There are plenty of wheat-free pastas available today. The following are the ones used in this book but there are still more to choose from and more are becoming available all the time.

100% SOBA are noodles made from just buckwheat flour and sea salt. Be warned, however, that there are a number of different grades of soba on the market and some of them do contain wheat, so read the ingredients list on the label carefully.

BUCKWHEAT PASTA comes as spirals and can be used in place of macaroni.

AGLUTELLA GLUTEN-FREE PASTA is made from corn, rice and potato flour and is available in two forms, spaghetti or macaroni.

STIR-FRY RICE NOODLES are made from just rice and water. They are perfect for creating stir-fry dishes, crispy fried noodles and for use in soup.

CORN PASTA SPIRALS can be used instead of macaroni. They remain firm when cooked and are therefore good for pasta salads.

CORN SPAGHETTI is available with or without parsley. It too has a good texture.

MILLET AND RICE PASTA has a delicate flavour that goes well in any pasta dish but it needs careful cooking. This applies also to RICE SPAGHETTI and LENTIL PASTA SHELLS.

Soya Products

SOYA BEANS contain anti-trypsin and must be fully cooked before use; they can then be used as other beans in savoury dishes.

SOYA ALTERNATIVE TO MILK: see under Milks and Milk Products.

SOYA FLOUR has been pre-cooked and is safe to use without further cooking. It can be used to replace eggs in enriched pastry and in batters and a little mixed with water can be used instead of egg for glazing pastry. It can also be added in small amounts to recipes to provide extra protein.

TAMARI is soya sauce which is wheat-free. The only ingredients are soya beans, water and sea salt. It is however a fermented product and is therefore unsuitable for a Candida Control Diet.

TOFU or BEANCURD comes in two types: silken tofu, which can be used to replace cream or yoghurt in desserts and sauces, and firm tofu which has a cheese-like consistency, is available both marinated and natural and is used diced in stir-fries. Both are useful for anyone on a Dairy-free Diet.

'CIRRUS WHOLE EGG REPLACER' is derived entirely from soya beans. For details see below under Egg Replacers.

'SOYA CREEM' can be very useful on a dairy-free diet. It has a large number of ingredients, so check the label to see if it is suitable.

N.B. Some soya products may contain genetically-modified material. If this is of concern it would be best to buy organic whenever possible.

Sweeteners

RAW CANE SUGAR. It appears that more people are sensitive to beet sugar than to cane and that is why many of the recipes in this book suggest using demerara sugar. As this is rather coarse-grained, some of the recipes recommend that the demerara sugar be ground in a liquidiser to give a consistency similar to castor sugar.

FRUCTOSE is about half as sweet again as ordinary sugar (sucrose).

GLUCOSE is not quite as sweet as sugar. This is reflected in the instructions given in the recipes.

HONEY. The types of honey recommended for those who cannot have sugar are Mexican, Chinese, African, Australian and any that are labelled tropical, as the bees are not fed on sugar during the winter as they are in temperate zones. When substituting honey for sugar in a recipe, use honey to the same measure recommended for sugar, but reduce the liquid content of the recipe by one quarter. Also cook at a slightly lower temperature. When adding honey to margarine, pour it slowly in a fine stream, blending well for better volume and texture.

MAPLE SYRUP, DATE SYRUP, RICE SYRUP and OAT SYRUP can all be used to replace golden syrup in most applications.

Egg Replacers

CIRRUS WHOLE EGG REPLACER is made from a blend of soya proteins and is 100% soya. It has been formulated primarily for use in cakes where its whipping and gelling properties are used to full advantage. It should always be folded in as the last ingredient to ensure a good spongy texture.

CIRRUS EGG WHITE REPLACER is a cellulose derivative and is used for meringues and desserts.

CIRRUS 'HPMC' EGG REPLACER is also a cellulose derivative and is used to bind. Useful mainly for savoury dishes such as vegetable burgers which are not successful without a binding agent.

CIRRUS EGG REPLACERS are only available by mail order (see page 19).

APRICOT EGG REPLACER and DATE EGG REPLACER (see page 189) have a very limited application where an egg would be used to bind. These are not suitable egg substitutes in recipes where aeration is required.

Milk and Milk Products

The milks used in this book to replace cows' milk are goats' milk, sheep's milk, soya milk, nut milk, coconut milk and 'Rice Dream'.

FRESH GOATS' MILK is the most commonly-used alternative to cows' milk. It is usually sold in 500ml or 1 pint packs; it has a similar fat content to cows' milk but the fat globules are smaller, making it easier to digest.

POWDERED GOATS' MILK (both whole and skimmed) is also

widely available.

FRESH SHEEP'S MILK has a higher fat content than cows' and goats' milk, making it highly valued for yoghurt and cheese making. Sheep's milk is also sold frozen in 500ml or 1 pint packs and is becoming easier to obtain.

POWDERED SHEEP'S MILK is also available.

SOYA ALTERNATIVE TO MILK (referred to in the recipes as soya milk) is the most commonly-used vegetable milk; it can be used as a substitute for animal milk in most applications and is widely available.

POWDERED SOYA MILK is also available.

NUT MILK can be made from any variety of nuts (see page 188), the only limitation being that if the milk is to be white then blanched almonds or cashews must be used.

COCONUT MILK is available in tins or is made from reconstituted creamed coconut.

'RICE DREAM' is a milk substitute made from rice. It is available in cartons, 'natural' or 'flavoured'. Use the 'natural' one for baking purposes.

All these milks are suitable for baking purposes and for serving with breakfast cereals.

WARNING: Do ensure that all dairy products are made from milk that has been pasteurised. Do not use any of these milks for young babies. Special formulae for babies are available on prescription from your doctor or hospital and weaning onto any of these milks should be done under the supervision of your doctor or health visitor.

GOATS' YOGHURT and SHEEP'S YOGHURT are both widely available.

Cheeses

It is important to ensure that whatever cheese is used is made with vegetarian rennet and is therefore free of any calf rennet.

GOATS' CHEDDAR is the most commonly available hard goats' cheese but any other may be used.

SOFT GOATS' CHEESES come in various forms, some softer than others. The soft cheese used in the recipes is of a cream cheese or curd cheese texture. This can be made using the recipe for Curd Cheese (see page 185).

SHEEP'S (EWES') CHEESES. These are now widely available and

come from a number of countries of origin. Any hard sheep's or ewes' cheeses made with vegetarian rennet may be used. Roquefort is a blue-veined sheep's cheese and Feta Cheese is also available made from sheep's milk. Some Feta Cheese does contain cows' milk, so check carefully before you buy.

SOFT SHEEP'S CHEESE can be made using the recipe for Curd Cheese (see page 185). This curd cheese is very useful in cooking and can be substituted for cottage cheese or cream cheese in a wide variety of recipes.

PARMAZANO is a grated soya cheese which is sold in little shaker dispensers. It is the dairy-free version of parmesan.

Margarines, Fats and Spreads

MARGARINE. The term 'milk-free margarine' is used throughout the book to denote any margarine which does not contain any cows' milk products of any kind. As most margarines contain whey, which is a product of cows' milk, it is necessary for anyone on a cows' milk-free diet to change to a milk-free margarine. There are several brands on the market containing oils from differing sources and so it should be possible to find one that suits your needs.

VEGETABLE FATS, of which there are a number available, are also very useful on a milk-free diet.

VEGETABLE SUET dusted with rice flour instead of wheat flour is gluten-free and therefore very useful.

SPREADS are an alternative to margarine and are made from nuts and seeds, which means they are also very nutritious. Almond Butter, Hazelnut Butter, Peanut Butter, Sunflower Spread, and Tahini (Sesame Spread) are all available sugar-free, or you can make nut butters and seed spreads by following the recipes given in the section 'Dairy Substitutes'.

Oils

There are a tremendous number of different kinds of edible oils to choose from and so in this book most recipes say 'oil of choice' rather than specifying a particular one. However, it needs to be said that the nutritional value of many oils is greatly reduced by cooking them. From a nutritional point of view, the best oils to use in cooking are olive oil or rice oil as they are not harmed by heat. On the other hand it is appreciated that many who use this book will be on (or catering for those who are on) very restricted diets and rotation diets. For the highest nutritional value use cold-pressed oils, but whatever oils you use do try to make sure that they are free from antioxidants or other additives and that they are as fresh as possible.

When converting from a recipe using margarine, reduce the fat content by one third, e.g. 170g (6 oz) margarine becomes 100 ml (4 fl oz) oil. Oil is not suitable for use where a solid fat is melted and used as a binding agent on cooling, as in flapjacks.

Sugar-free Fruit Spreads

These are sugar-free jams which are made from concentrated fruit juices and fruit pulp. They are a boon to anyone on a sugar-free diet and a healthier alternative for everyone.

Eggs

Eggs, too, should be consumed when really fresh and wherever possible should be free-range or, better still, organic. Many people who are allergic to 'Battery' eggs are not allergic to eggs from hens that are both free-range and additive-free.

If you have duck, goose, bantam or quail eggs, use them by weight, bearing in mind that a standard hen's egg weighs 50g (2 oz) without its shell.

Natural Colours

Over the past few years many food manufacturers have gone over to using natural colours instead of artificial ones in their products. It is still important to read ingredients lists carefully to avoid artificial colours but you should have no difficulty in finding a naturally-coloured version of most products.

Other Ingredients

There are various other ingredients not mentioned above that have been used in these recipes. Each one has been carefully chosen for a specific reason. Examples are:

GREEN AND BLACK'S ORGANIC DARK CHOCOLATE is not only milk-free and organic but also is sweetened with raw cane sugar. PLAMIL CAROB CONFECTION is a good alternative to chocolate, is dairy-free and contains no sugar at all.
BROWN RICE VINEGAR is gluten-free.
CIDER VINEGAR is grain-free.
KALLO YEAST-FREE VEGETABLE STOCK CUBES are the most widely available stock cubes suitable for use on a Candida albicans Control Diet.
'SUMA' TINNED BEANS, CHICK PEAS AND LENTILS are salt- and sugar-free and they are prepared in filtered water.

Preservatives (e.g. Sulphur Dioxide)

Preservatives are commonly found in many foods. As with other additives these can cause problems for sensitive individuals. Dried fruits in particular often contain sulphur dioxide. If the fruits have a good colour then it is likely that they contain it. Naturally-dried fruits are much darker in colour (particularly sultanas, apricots, peaches, apples and pears). Preservatives are also commonly found in the following foods unless they specifically state that they are free of preservatives: glacé cherries, candied peel, crystallised fruits, desiccated coconut, frozen fruit pulp or purée, beer, cider, wine, some fruit juices (including concentrated grape juice for home winemaking), some cider vinegars, liquid pectin, golden syrup, dried vegetables, hamburgers, sausages, frozen mushrooms, powdered garlic, and some jellies.

* * *

All the recipes serve four persons unless otherwise stated, and all the spoon measurements given are level.

Some Useful Addresses

Ceres Natural Foods, 42 Princes Street, Yeovil, Somerset BA20 1EQ. Tel. 01935 428791. Retail and mail order supplier of natural food products and supplements. A wide range of special-needs foods and ingredients including unusual flours.

Cirrus Associates (S.W.), Little Hintock, Kington Magna, Gillingham, Dorset SP8 5EW. Tel. 01747 838165. Mail order supplier of Cirrus egg replacers and 'Arise' raising agent. Also appliances such as waffle makers, stainless steel jug kettles, VDU screens and antennae, and other items suitable for environmentally sensitive people.

Infinity Foods Cooperative Ltd., 25 North Road, Brighton, Sussex BN1 1YA. Tel. 01273 603563. Retail stockist of a wide range of organic and natural foods. If you do not live in the area, your local health food shop should be able to order specialist items for you from their wholesale warehouse (Tel. 01273 424060).

Itona Ltd., Leyland Mill Lane, Wigan, Lancs WN1 2SB. Tel. 01942 234761. They can supply amaranth products (whole seeds, toasted flour and crunchy flakes) and other specialist foods.

Breakfast Cereals

Buckwheat Porridge

Serves 2

75g (3 oz) buckwheat flakes
700ml (24 fl oz) water

Pinch of salt

Stir buckwheat flakes into water in a saucepan and add a pinch of salt. Bring to the boil. Simmer, stirring occasionally, for about 5 minutes.

Maizemeal Porridge (Polenta)
Serves 2

135g (4½ oz) maizemeal   *Pinch of salt*
700ml (24 fl oz) water

Blend maizemeal with a cupful of the measured water to a smooth paste. Bring rest of water to the boil in a non-stick or heavy-based saucepan. Stir in maizemeal mixture and bring back to the boil, stirring all the time until it is smooth; this prevents it sticking to the bottom of the pan. Cover and simmer very gently for 15 minutes.
Cold leftovers will set and can be sliced, coated in maizemeal and fried in olive oil or corn oil.

 # Millet Porridge
Serves 2

115g (4 oz) millet flakes   *425ml (¾ pt) water*

Combine millet flakes with water in saucepan and bring to the boil, stirring all the time until the mixture thickens. Remove from heat. Cover tightly, and stand in a warm place for 10 minutes. Stir before serving.

 # Whole Millet Cereal

850ml (1½ pt) water   *30ml (2 tbsp) oil of choice*
200g (7 oz) whole millet   *Salt to taste*

Boil the water and then add millet, oil and salt. Bring back to the boil, cover and simmer for 20 minutes or until millet is cooked and has absorbed the water.
Use for breakfast as a porridge with honey and a milk of choice or with a main meal instead of potato or rice.
Cold leftovers will set and can be sliced and fried.

Quick Oat Porridge
Serves 2

75g (3 oz) porridge oats   *Pinch of salt*
700ml (24 fl oz) water

Put porridge oats and water in a saucepan, and add a pinch of salt. Bring to the boil and continue boiling for 1 minute, stirring all the time.

 # Oatmeal Porridge
Serves 2

500ml (18 fl oz) water   *50g (2 oz) medium oatmeal*
Pinch of salt

Pour the water into a saucepan and bring it to the boil. When it is boiling hard, sprinkle the oatmeal in slowly to prevent lumps forming. After five minutes, when the oatmeal is slightly swollen, cover with a lid and simmer for about 30 minutes, stirring frequently. Season to taste.

 # Brown Rice Porridge
Serves 2

135g (4½ oz) brown rice   *500ml (18 fl oz) water*
  flakes   *Pinch of salt*

Stir brown rice flakes into water in a saucepan and bring to the boil. Simmer, stirring occasionally, for 5–10 minutes. Season.

 # Popcorn
Serves 1

10ml (2 tsp) popping corn   *10ml (2 tsp) oil of choice*

Place oil in a frying pan and heat slightly to disperse oil over the bottom of the pan. Add popping corn and immediately cover with a lid. Turn up heat to high. When you hear the first grains popping give the pan a shake. Return to heat and continue to cook until the popping stops. Remove from heat immediately and serve.

 # Fresh Fruit Cereal
Serves 1

1 dessert apple or pear
15–30ml (1–2 tbsp) oat bran
   and oat germ

1 kiwi fruit or other fresh
   fruit in season

Grate the apple or pear into a cereal bowl and add sufficient oat bran and oat germ for the mixture to stick together but not be too dry. Decorate the top with a sliced kiwi fruit or other fresh fruit. Serve immediately.

 # Apricot Cereal
Serves 1

75g (3 oz) porridge oats,
   millet or buckwheat flakes

40–50g (1½–2 oz)
   unsulphured dried apricots

Put the apricots in a basin with just enough water to cover and leave to soak overnight. Just before serving put the flakes into a cereal bowl and mix with some of the apricot liquor. Top with drained apricots.

Gl Use millet flakes or buckwheat flakes.
Gr Use buckwheat flakes.

 # Prune Cereal
Serves 1

Follow recipe and method for 'Apricot Cereal', substituting unsorbated prunes for unsulphured dried apricots.

See Dietary Notes given for 'Apricot Cereal'.

Crunchy Oat Granola

450g (1 lb) porridge oats
115g (4 oz) oat bran and
  oat germ
115g (4 oz) walnuts or
  pecans, chopped
50g (2 oz) flaked almonds
  or flaked hazelnuts
50g (2 oz) sesame seeds

30ml (2 tbsp) lemon rind,
  grated
60ml (4 tbsp) vegetable oil
60ml (4 tbsp) malt extract
  or oat syrup
175g (6 oz) natural raisins
  or natural sultanas

In a large bowl mix together the porridge oats, oat bran and germ, nuts, seeds and lemon rind. In a small bowl stir together the oil and malt extract or oat syrup. Pour this mixture over the dry ingredients and stir well until evenly mixed. Spread the mixture over a large baking sheet and bake at 150°C, 300°F, Gas Mark 2, stirring frequently, until golden and crunchy. Remove from oven and cool. Then stir in raisins or sultanas. When completely cold, store in an airtight container.

Gluten-Free Granola

275g (10 oz) millet flakes
275g (10 oz) buckwheat
  flakes
115g (4 oz) cashews,
  chopped
25g (1 oz) flaked almonds
  or flaked hazelnuts
50g (2 oz) sesame seeds

30ml (2 tbsp) lemon rind,
  grated
60ml (4 tbsp) vegetable oil
75ml (5 tbsp) maple syrup
175g (6 oz) natural raisins
  or natural sultanas

Method as for 'Crunchy Oat Granola'.

Breads, Plain and Fancy, Scones and Teacakes

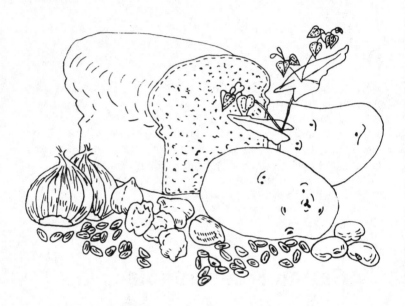

⊞E Rye Bread

575g (1 lb 4 oz) rye flour
5ml (1 tsp) salt
10ml (2 tsp) demerara sugar
300ml (½ pt) lukewarm water

15ml (1 tbsp) dried yeast
or 40g (1½ oz) fresh yeast
15ml (1 tbsp) oil of choice

Place flour and salt in a bowl with 5ml (1 tsp) sugar and mix well. Put remaining sugar and yeast into a jug and add the lukewarm water and mix well. If using dried yeast stand the jug in a warm place for 10 minutes until contents are frothy. Add yeast liquid and oil to flour and mix to a soft dough, adding a little more liquid if necessary. Turn onto a lightly floured surface and knead well for 5 minutes. Place in a bowl, cover with a damp cloth and leave to rise in a warm place until doubled in size. Re-knead and divide dough into two pieces. Shape each piece and place in well-oiled 500g (1 lb) loaf tins. Cover with a damp cloth and leave to rise until doubled in size again. Bake at 230°C, 450°F, Gas Mark 8 for about 40 minutes.

Barley Bread

15ml (1 tbsp) dried yeast
10ml (2 tsp) black treacle
  or honey
675g (1 lb 8 oz) barley flour

5ml (1 tsp) salt
450ml (16 fl oz) lukewarm
  water
15ml (1 tbsp) oil of choice

Put yeast and sweetener of choice in a little extra warm water and set aside to froth. Warm flour in mixing bowl, stir in salt and then add the frothed yeast. Add the oil to the lukewarm water and mix to make a dough. Knead well, put into a bowl and cover with a damp cloth. Leave to rise in a warm place for about 1½–2 hours, until doubled in size. Knock back and knead again. Place on an oiled baking tray and leave to prove for up to an hour, covered and in a warm place. Make a deep cut along the top of the loaf and open it out with the side of the hand. Bake at 200°C, 400°F, Gas Mark 6 for approximately 1 hour.

Potato and Rice Bread

5ml (1 tsp) sugar or 2·5ml
  (½ tsp) fructose
20ml (4 tsp) dried yeast
300ml (½ pt) hand-hot
  water

275g (10 oz) potato flour
225g (8 oz) brown rice flour
2·5–5ml (½–1 tsp) salt
15ml (1 tbsp) oil of choice

Put the sugar or fructose, dried yeast and hand-hot water into a jug and leave in a warm place until froth is about 2·5cm (1") deep. Mix flours and salt in a large bowl. Add yeast mixture and oil and mix to a thick batter adding more hand-hot water as necessary. Oil two 500g (1 lb) loaf tins liberally and flour freely to prevent loaves sticking to tins. Divide mixture between the two tins. Leave to rise in a warm place for 20–30 minutes. (Potato flour rises well so do not leave it to rise for too long or the loaves will be full of holes.) Bake at 230°C, 450°F, Gas Mark 8 for 35–40 minutes.

Potato and Buckwheat Bread

Follow recipe and method for 'Potato and Rice Bread' substituting the flours used in the following proportions:

275g (10 oz) potato flour   *225g (8 oz) buckwheat flour*

Potato and Chestnut Bread

Follow recipe and method for 'Potato and Rice Bread' substituting the flours used in the following proportions:

350g (12 oz) potato flour   *175g (6 oz) chestnut flour*

Rice and Chestnut Bread

Follow recipe and method for 'Potato and Rice Bread' substituting the flours used in the following proportions:

350g (12 oz) brown rice flour   *175g (6 oz) chestnut flour*

Buckwheat and Rice Bread

Follow recipe and method for 'Potato and Rice Bread' substituting the flours used in the following proportions:

350g (12 oz) buckwheat flour   *175g (6 oz) brown rice flour*

Amaranth Bread

Follow recipe and method for 'Potato and Rice Bread' substituting the flours used in the following proportions:

350g (12 oz) potato flour
  or brown rice flour

175g (6 oz) toasted
  amaranth flour

 Use potato flour.

Potato and Soya Bread

15g (½ oz) dried yeast
5ml (1 tsp) sugar
115ml (4 fl oz) lukewarm
  water
115g (4 oz) potato flour

60ml (4 tbsp) soya flour
Pinch of salt
30ml (2 tbsp) soya bran
15ml (1 tbsp) soya oil
1 egg, lightly beaten

Mix yeast with sugar, add some of the water and leave to froth. Sieve potato flour, soya flour and salt into a bowl and then stir in the soya bran and oil. Mix to a thick batter with yeast mixture, egg and the rest of the water. Place in a 500g (1 lb) loaf tin which has been oiled and floured with potato flour and leave to rise. Bake at 200°C, 400°F, Gas Mark 6 for 15 minutes and then turn down to 180°C, 350°F, Gas Mark 4 for a further 15–20 minutes. Turn out onto wire rack to cool.

Mixed Flour Bread

300ml (½ pt) lukewarm water
15g (½ oz) dried yeast
2 eating apples or pears
50g (2 oz) milk-free margarine
  or 30ml (2 tbsp) oil of choice
240g (8½ oz) brown rice flour
  or potato flour
50g (2 oz) soya flour

25g (1 oz) maizemeal, millet
  flakes or millet flour
25g (1 oz) chick pea flour
  or buckwheat flour
Pinch of salt
15g (½ oz) ground almonds
  or ground hazelnuts

If using millet flakes, place in blender, turn into flour and set aside. Put the lukewarm water into the blender and sprinkle the dried yeast into it. Slice the apples or pears, put into the blender with the yeast and water and blend. Melt the margarine, if using. Put all the dry ingredients into a large mixing bowl and add the melted margarine or oil. Stir well with a wooden spoon. Add the yeast mixture and stir very well to make a batter. Turn into two greased or oiled 500g (1 lb) loaf tins and bake at 180°C, 350°F, Gas Mark 4 near the top of the oven for 40–45 minutes. Store wrapped in the fridge for up to 2 days or freeze.

The fruit in this recipe greatly improves the keeping quality, however it is still a good idea to freeze the second loaf to ensure its freshness.

⊞E̶ Sultana or Raisin Bread

Add 10ml (2 tsp) fructose or 20ml (4 tsp) sugar to the previous recipe along with 50g (2 oz) natural sultanas or raisins before the final mixing.

⊞E̶ Millet Fruit Loaf

*115g (4 oz) natural sultanas
or natural raisins
300ml (½ pt) boiling water
15g (½ oz) dried yeast
75g (3 oz) potato flour*

*50g (2 oz) soya flour
225g (8 oz) millet flakes or
millet flour
50ml (2 fl oz) oil of choice*

If using millet flakes, place them in a blender, turn into flour and set aside. Soak dried fruit in 300ml (½ pt) boiling water for 15 minutes. Transfer to blender or food processor, blend and then check for temperature. Reheat to hand-hot if necessary. Stir in yeast and leave for about 10 minutes until frothy. Put flours together in a large mixing bowl and add yeast mixture and oil. Mix well with a wooden spoon and pour into 2 oiled 500g (1 lb) loaf tins. Bake at 180°C, 350°F, Gas Mark 4 for 40–45 minutes.

⊞E̶ Chick Pea Bread

*5ml (1 tsp) sugar
20ml (4 tsp) dried yeast
500ml (18 fl oz) hand-hot
water*

*500g (18 oz) chick pea flour
5ml (1 tsp) salt
50g (2 oz) milk-free
margarine*

Put the sugar or fructose, dried yeast and hand-hot water into a jug and leave in a warm place until froth is about 2·5cm (1") deep. Mix flour and salt in a large bowl. Add margarine and rub into the flour. Add yeast mixture and mix to a thick batter adding more hand-hot water, if necessary. Grease two 500g (1 lb) loaf tins liberally and flour freely with chick pea flour to prevent loaves sticking to the tins. Divide mixture between the two tins. Leave to rise in a warm place for 20–30 minutes. Bake at 230°C, 450°F, Gas Mark 8 for 35–40 minutes.

Notes on Gluten-free Breads

Gluten-free breads should be eaten freshly-made or frozen until required as they quickly go stale. All of them make good croutons or toast and if frozen sliced may be toasted straight from the freezer.

The dough is not like wheat dough but is more like a thick batter. Some flours absorb more water than others, therefore extra water has to be added where necessary. Most of the recipes make two loaves, one to use freshly-baked and the other to freeze.

Breadcrumbs made from any of these yeast breads, soda breads, batter breads or plain scones can be used for savoury dishes; see various recipes between pages 137–164.

 # Olive Bread

Use any of the plain yeast breads or soda breads in this chapter. To every 450g (1 lb) flour add the following ingredients: 30ml (2 tbsp) mixed fresh herbs, chopped, 30ml (2 tbsp) olive oil and 150g (5 oz) stoned black olives in brine, well drained.

See Dietary Notes given for the chosen bread recipe.

C E Gl Gr Herb Bread

Use any of the plain yeast breads, soda breads or scones in this chapter. To every 450g (1 lb) flour add the following ingredients: 90–150ml (6–10 tbsp) mixed fresh herbs, finely chopped, according to taste. Suggested proportions: 45–60ml (3–4 tbsp) parsley and 15ml (1 tbsp) strongly flavoured herbs such as thyme, marjoram, basil or oregano. 1 crushed clove of garlic can also be added.

See Dietary Notes given for the chosen bread recipe.

C E Gl Gr Tomato and Thyme Bread

Use any of the plain yeast breads, soda breads or scones in this chapter. To every 450g (1 lb) flour add the following ingredients: 50g (2 oz) bottled sun-dried tomatoes in olive oil, drained and chopped. Soak the tomatoes in 200ml (7 fl oz) boiling water for 15 minutes. Drain and reserve liquor for use in vegetable stock. Add the rehydrated tomatoes to the dough together with 1 egg and 15ml (1 tbsp) fresh thyme, chopped.

See Dietary Notes given for the chosen bread recipe.

C E Rye Soda Bread

This recipe uses the Irish way of making soda bread with soured milk. This gives a good rise and therefore a softer texture.

10ml (2 tsp) lemon juice
575ml (1 pt) goats' milk
* or sheep's milk*
675g (1 lb 8 oz) rye flour

15ml (3 tsp) bicarbonate
* of soda*
Pinch of salt
30ml (2 tbsp) olive oil

Put the lemon juice in the milk and leave for up to 15 minutes. Place the flour, bicarbonate of soda and salt in a mixing bowl and mix well. Add the soured milk and oil and mix to a soft dough.

Turn out onto a well floured surface and cover the dough with more flour to make it easier to handle. Place on a baking sheet and flatten top with hands. Form into a 23cm (9") round loaf. Score loaf into eight equal-sized wedges. Bake at 190°C, 375°F, Gas Mark 5 for 30 minutes.

C Can be made without the lemon, if lemon is not allowed.

CE Barley Soda Bread

Follow recipe and method for 'Rye Soda Bread' substituting barley flour for rye flour.

See Dietary Note given for 'Rye Soda Bread'.

CE 'Arise' Bread

'Arise' is a raising agent which, when used in conjunction with bicarbonate of soda, will produce yeast-free bread of excellent volume and texture. A mixture of sodium bicarbonate and potassium bicarbonate (2:1) can be used, if preferred.

450g (1 lb) rye flour or barley flour	*40g (1½ oz) 'Arise'*
15g (½ oz) bicarbonate of soda	*5ml (1 tsp) salt*
	300ml (10 fl oz) water
	25g (1 oz) vegetable fat

Grease and flour a 1kg (2 lb) loaf tin. Put all the dry ingredients into the bowl of a mixer with a dough hook (e.g. Kenwood Chef), and add the water and vegetable fat. Mix slowly for about 5 minutes to develop the dough. The dough consistency should not be sticky so add a little more flour if it is necessary. Roll out the dough to an oblong 1·25cm (½") thick and roll up like a Swiss Roll. Put into prepared loaf tin and bake immediately at 220°C, 425°F, Gas Mark 7 for about 40 minutes.

Potato Soda Bread

115g (4 oz) potato flour
60ml (4 tbsp) soya flour
10ml (2 tsp) gluten-free
  baking powder or 2·5ml
  (½ tsp) bicarbonate of soda
Pinch of salt
115ml (4 fl oz) water

15–30ml (1–2 tbsp) soya
  bran
25g (1 oz) milk-free
  margarine or 15ml
  (1 tbsp) oil of choice
1 egg, beaten

Sieve together potato flour, soya flour, baking powder or bicarbonate of soda and salt and then stir in the soya bran. Rub in margarine or oil. Add beaten egg and water and whisk or beat to a smooth batter. Pour into an oiled and bottom-lined 500g (1 lb) loaf tin and bake at 200°C, 400°F, Gas Mark 6 for about 35 minutes. Turn out onto wire rack to cool.

 **Potato Soda Bread
(Soya- and Egg-free)**

65ml (2½ fl oz) 'Cirrus
  Egg White Replacer'
  (5% solution)
115ml (4 fl oz) water
Pinch of salt
225g (8 oz) potato flour

20ml (4 tsp) gluten-free
  baking powder or 5ml
  (1 tsp) bicarbonate of soda
120ml (8 tbsp) any nuts,
  finely ground
30ml (2 tbsp) oil of choice

Put egg white replacer solution, water and salt into a bowl and whisk vigorously until it stands in stiff peaks. Sieve together potato flour and baking powder or bicarbonate of soda. Add to whisked solution along with rest of ingredients and beat to a smooth paste with a wooden spoon. Put into well-oiled loaf tin and bake at 200°C, 400°F, Gas Mark 6 for about 35 minutes. Turn onto wire rack to cool.
Eat the same day.

Millet Bread

115g (4 oz) millet flour or
    millet flakes
1 carrot, grated
15ml (1 tbsp) clear honey
    or maple syrup
Pinch of salt

30ml (2 tbsp) oil of choice
225ml (8 fl oz) boiling
    water
2 eggs
30ml (2 tbsp) cold water

If using millet flakes, place them in a blender and turn into flour. Combine the millet flour, carrot, honey or maple syrup, salt and oil in a bowl. Mix well. Stir in boiling water. Separate the eggs, beat the yolks well and add 30ml (2 tbsp) cold water and continue to beat. Add to flour mixture. Fold in stiffly-beaten egg whites. Place the batter in an oiled oblong baking tin and bake at 180°C, 350°F, Gas Mark 4 for about 40 minutes.

Rice, Soya and Raisin Bread

60ml (4 tbsp) soya milk
2 eggs
60ml (4 tbsp) sugar or honey
60ml (4 tbsp) soya oil
175g (6 oz) brown rice flour
50g (2 oz) soya flour

10ml (2 tsp) gluten-free
    baking powder or 2·5ml
    (½ tsp) bicarbonate of soda
50g (2 oz) natural raisins
25g (1 oz) any nuts, finely
    chopped

Mix milk, eggs, sugar or honey and oil. Sieve dry ingredients and gradually blend into the mixture. Stir in the raisins and nuts. Pour into a well-oiled loaf tin and leave to rest for 1 hour. Bake at 180°C, 350°F, Gas Mark 4 for 45 minutes.

Malt Loaf

60ml (4 tbsp) malt extract
60ml (4 tbsp) maple syrup
40g (1½ oz) milk-free
    margarine
1 egg or 15g (½ oz) 'Cirrus
    Whole Egg Replacer' and
    45ml (3 tbsp) water

90ml (6 tbsp) goats' milk,
    sheep's milk or soya milk
225g (8 oz) barley flour
5ml (1 tsp) bicarbonate
    of soda
115g (4 oz) natural raisins
Pinch of salt

Grease and bottom-line a 1kg (2 lb) loaf tin. Measure maple syrup and malt extract carefully, levelling off spoon with a knife. Place in a saucepan together with the margarine and melt over gentle heat.

For loaf made with egg:
Put egg in a bowl with the milk and whisk. Place dry ingredients in a large bowl and stir in raisins. Make a well in the centre and add all the rest of the ingredients at the same time. Beat well with a wooden spoon until smooth.

For loaf made with whole egg replacer:
Put whole egg replacer in a small basin with the 45ml (3 tbsp) water and whisk with a rotary beater until fluffy. Fold in the whipped whole egg replacer as last ingredient.

Put mixture into prepared tin and level off the top. Bake in centre of oven at 160°C, 325°F, Gas Mark 3 for 1–1¼ hours. Test with a knife to make sure centre is completely cooked. Leave in the tin for 5–10 minutes and then turn out onto a wire rack until cold. Store in an airtight tin. The flavour develops on keeping.

E Use *'Cirrus Whole Egg Replacer'*.

 # Date and Walnut Loaf

75g (3 oz) potato flour
75g (3 oz) buckwheat flour
15ml (3 tsp) gluten-free
   baking powder
Pinch of salt
2·5ml (½ tsp) bicarbonate
   of soda
40g (1½ oz) walnuts, chopped
50g (2 oz) dates, chopped

60ml (4 tbsp) date syrup
20g (¾ oz) milk-free
   margarine
150ml (¼ pt) goats' milk,
   sheep's milk or soya milk
1 egg or 15g (½ oz) 'Cirrus
   Whole Egg Replacer' and
   45ml (3 tbsp) water

Grease and line a 500g (1 lb) loaf tin. Sieve the flours, baking powder, salt and bicarbonate of soda into a mixing bowl. Stir in the walnuts and chopped dates. Warm the date syrup, margarine and milk together until the margarine melts.

For loaf made with egg:
Whisk the egg in a separate bowl and add to the dry ingredients along with the warmed mixture.

For loaf made with whole egg replacer:
Put 45ml (3 tbsp) water into a small mixing bowl, add the whole egg replacer and whisk until fluffy. Stir the warmed liquid into the flours and then gradually fold in the whisked whole egg replacer.

Pour into prepared tin and bake at 180°C, 350°F, Gas Mark 4 for 1 hour or until well-risen and firm. Turn onto a cooling rack, remove paper and leave until quite cold. Serve sliced and spread with milk-free margarine.

E Use *'Cirrus Whole Egg Replacer'*.

Maizemeal Bread

225g (8 oz) maizemeal
5ml (1 tsp) bicarbonate of
　soda
Pinch of salt

300ml (½ pt) goats' milk,
　sheep's milk or soya milk
45ml (3 tbsp) corn oil
1 egg

Brush a 23x18cm (9x7") tin with corn oil. Place all ingredients together in a blender or food processor and blend well. Pour into prepared tin. Bake at 220°C, 425°F, Gas Mark 7 for 20–25 minutes or until golden brown. Cut into squares while still in the tin and then transfer to a wire rack to cool.

Millet Batter Bread

Follow recipe and method for 'Maizemeal Bread' substituting millet flour or millet flakes for maizemeal. If using millet flakes, place them in a blender and turn into flour.

Brown Rice Batter Bread

Follow recipe and method for 'Maizemeal Bread' substituting brown rice flour for maizemeal.

Banana Batter Bread

Follow recipe and method for 'Maizemeal Bread' substituting banana flour for maizemeal and olive oil for corn oil.

 # Rice Scone Bread

5ml (1 tsp) lemon juice
300ml (½ pt) goats' milk
  or sheep's milk
350g (12 oz) brown rice flour
Pinch of salt

7·5ml (1½ tsp) bicarbonate
  of soda
1 egg, beaten
15ml (1 tbsp) olive oil

Put the lemon juice in the milk and leave for up to 15 minutes. Place the flour, salt and bicarbonate of soda in a mixing bowl and mix well. Add soured milk, beaten egg and oil and mix to a soft dough. Turn out onto a floured surface, cover dough with flour and gently form into a round loaf. Place on a baking sheet and flatten top with hands. Score loaf into four equal-sized wedges. Bake at 190°C, 375°F, Gas Mark 5 for 30 minutes.

C If allowed lemon.

 # Tomato- and Onion-topped Rice Scone Bread

1 quantity Rice Scone Bread
  (previous recipe)
4 ripe tomatoes
15ml (1 tbsp) olive oil
2 onions, sliced

1 clove garlic, crushed
15ml (1 tbsp) feta
  cheese, finely diced
15ml (1 tbsp) fresh
  oregano, chopped

Peel tomatoes, remove seeds and chop into small dice. Heat the oil in a pan and sauté onions and garlic until onion is soft. Add tomatoes, cheese and oregano. Cook for 5 minutes, stirring the whole time. Cover with a lid and simmer until tomatoes are softened. Allow mixture to cool. Place the dough on a baking sheet, flatten top with hands and score with a large cross on the top. Open the cross shape out with the side of the hand and fill the depression with the tomato and onion mixture. Bake at 190°C, 375°F, Gas Mark 5 for 30 minutes.

C E Corn and Rye Tortillas

In Mexico and Ecuador tortillas are traditionally served with a chilli and bean casserole. Variations on these flat breads can be found in many cuisines throughout the world.

135g (4½ oz) maizemeal   *75ml (5 tbsp) corn oil*
135g (4½ oz) rye flour   *225ml (8 fl oz) water*
2·5ml (½ tsp) salt   *(approx.)*

Mix flours and salt and stir in the oil. Add water gradually until it forms a soft, slightly sticky dough. Knead well. Place in a bowl and cover for about ½ hour. Roll out walnut-sized pieces on a rye-floured surface into circles about 13cm (5") in diameter. Cook tortillas in an ungreased frying pan or on a griddle. Allow to cook until bubbles appear and then turn over and cook the other side. Once cooked, keep warm in a covered dish in the oven until the whole batch is cooked.

C E Barley Scones

450g (1 lb) barley flour   *300ml (½ pt) goats' milk,*
10ml (2 tsp) bicarbonate of soda   *sheep's milk, soya milk*
115g (4 oz) milk-free margarine   *or water*
or 60ml (4 tbsp) oil of choice

Sieve flour and bicarbonate of soda into a bowl. Rub in the margarine or oil. Add the milk or water all at once, and mix to a soft dough. Turn onto a floured surface and knead dough lightly until smooth. Roll out to about 1·25cm (½") thickness and cut into 6·5cm (2½") rounds. Transfer to a greased or oiled baking tray. Brush tops with milk of choice, if liked. Bake at top of oven at 230°C, 450°F, Gas Mark 8 for 7–10 minutes.

⌈C⌉⌈E⌉ Rye Scones

Follow recipe and method for 'Barley Scones' substituting rye flour for barley flour.

⌈⌉⌈E⌉/⌈Gl⌉⌈Gr⌉ Sago Scones

225g (8 oz) sago flour
20ml (4 tsp) gluten-free
  baking powder or 5ml
  (1 tsp) bicarbonate of soda
50g (2 oz) milk-free
  margarine or 30ml
  (2 tbsp) oil of choice

25g (1 oz) sugar or 15g
  (½ oz) fructose
115ml (4 fl oz) goats' milk,
  sheep's milk or soya milk
  or water

Sieve flour and baking powder or bicarbonate of soda into a bowl. Rub in the margarine or oil, then add sugar or fructose. Add milk or water all at once, and mix to a soft dough. Turn onto a floured surface and knead dough quickly until smooth. Roll out to about 1·25cm (½") thickness and cut into 5cm (2") rounds. Transfer to a greased or oiled baking tray. Bake at top of oven at 230°C, 450°F, Gas Mark 8 for 7–10 minutes. Cool on wire rack. Eat the same day.

⌈C⌉⌈E⌉/⌈Gl⌉⌈Gr⌉ Banana Scones

225g (8 oz) banana flour
20ml (4 tsp) gluten-free
  baking powder or 5ml
  (1 tsp) bicarbonate of soda
30ml (2 tbsp) oil of choice

25g (1 oz) demerara sugar
  (optional)
Up to 175ml (6 fl oz)
  goats' milk, sheep's milk,
  soya milk or water

Put the dry ingredients into a bowl and stir in the oil. Work in the liquid until sufficient has been added to form a stiff but pliable dough. Roll out on banana flour and cut into rounds with a 6·5cm (2½") cutter. Put on a baking tray and bake at 230°C, 450°F, Gas Mark 8 for 10 minutes. Eat while still hot.

⌈C⌉ Omit sugar.

C E Gl Gr Chick Pea Scones

250g (9 oz) chick pea flour
20ml (4 tsp) gluten-free
baking powder or 5ml
(1 tsp) bicarbonate of soda

50g (2 oz) milk-free
margarine
25g (1 oz) sugar or 15g
(½ oz) fructose (optional)
150ml (¼ pt) water

Sieve flour and baking powder or bicarbonate of soda into a bowl. Rub in margarine and then add sugar or fructose (if using them). Add water all at once and mix to a soft dough. Turn onto a well-floured surface and knead, using extra flour as necessary, until smooth. Roll out to about 1·25cm (½") thickness and cut into 5cm (2") rounds. Transfer to a baking tray and bake at the top of the oven at 230°C, 450°F, Gas Mark 8 for 10 minutes. Cool on wire rack. Eat the same day, preferably while still hot.

C Omit sugar or fructose.

C E Gl Gr Chestnut and Potato Scones

150g (5 oz) potato flour
115g (4 oz) chestnut flour
20ml (4 tsp) gluten-free baking
powder or 5ml (1 tsp) bicarb-
onate of soda

50g (2 oz) milk-free
margarine or 30ml
(2 tbsp) oil of choice
25g (1 oz) sugar or 15g
(½ oz) fructose (optional)
150ml (¼ pt) water

Sieve flours and baking powder or bicarbonate of soda into a bowl. Rub in margarine or stir in oil, then add sugar or fructose, if using. Add water all at once and mix to a soft dough. Turn onto a well-floured surface and knead using more flour if necessary until smooth. Roll out to about 1·25cm (½") thickness and cut into 5cm (2") rounds. Transfer to a greased baking tray and bake at top of oven at 230°C, 450°F, Gas Mark 8 for 7–10 minutes. Cool on a wire rack.

C Omit sugar or fructose.

Buckwheat and Potato Scones

Follow recipe and method for 'Chestnut and Potato Scones' substituting buckwheat flour for chestnut flour.

C Omit sugar or fructose.

Buckwheat Scones

225g (8 oz) buckwheat flakes
5ml (1 tsp) bicarbonate of soda
65ml (2½ fl oz) 'Nut Milk' (see page 188) or soya milk

15ml (1 tbsp) sunflower oil
15ml (1 tbsp) maple syrup

Place the buckwheat flakes in a blender and turn into a coarse flour. Mix the bicarbonate of soda with the milk. Mix all the ingredients together well. Roll into 8 balls with the palms of the hands and place them on a baking sheet. Flatten the tops and bake at 230°C, 450°F, Gas Mark 8 for 10 minutes.

Teacakes

175g (6 oz) chick pea flour
175g (6 oz) potato flour
50g (2 oz) arrowroot
25g (1 oz) buckwheat flour
25g (1 oz) chestnut flour
25ml (5 tsp) gluten-free baking powder

150g (5 oz) natural currants
75g (3 oz) natural sultanas
50g (2 oz) cashews or almonds
150ml (5 fl oz) cold water
15ml (1 tbsp) honey or maple syrup
200ml (7 fl oz) hot water

Sieve flours and baking powder into a large mixing bowl. Stir in the dried fruit. Put nuts and cold water into a blender and blend until smooth. Dissolve honey or maple syrup in hot water and add both liquids to the flours and mix well. Can be cooked in individual Yorkshire pudding tins or sandwich tins, according to the size of the teacakes required. Oil the tins and dust with sieved chick pea flour. Pour the mixture into the tins and smooth sides and top with the back of a spoon. Bake at 200°C, 400°F, Gas Mark 6 for about 25 minutes. Can be eaten immediately or frozen when cold and toasted straight from the freezer.

 # Millet and Rice Knobs

115g (4 oz) millet flour
or millet flakes
100g (3½ oz) brown rice flour
20ml (4 tsp) gluten-free
baking powder or 5ml
(1 tsp) bicarbonate of soda
Pinch of salt

15g (½ oz) ground almonds
or ground cashews
50g (2 oz) vegetable suet
with rice flour
150ml (5 fl oz) goats' milk,
sheep's milk, soya milk
or 'Rice Dream'

If using millet flakes, place in a blender and turn into flour. Mix flours and baking powder or bicarbonate of soda together in a bowl. Stir in the salt, ground nuts, and vegetable suet. Mix to a soft dough with the milk. Put spoonfuls into greased or oiled bun tins and bake at 230°C, 450°F, Gas Mark 8 for 10 minutes. Cool on wire rack.

Chick Pea Muffins

275g (10 oz) chick pea flour
15ml (3 tsp) gluten-free
baking powder
Pinch of salt
60ml (4 tbsp) maple syrup
200ml (7 fl oz) 'Nut Milk' (see
page 188)

30ml (2 tbsp) oil of choice
50g (2 oz) natural sultanas
or natural raisins
60ml (4 tbsp) 'Apricot Egg
Replacer' or 'Date Egg
Replacer' (see page 189)

Oil 12 muffin cups or bun tins. Put all the dry ingredients into a bowl. Add the rest of the ingredients and mix well. Put the mixture into the prepared tins and bake at 220°C, 425°F, Gas Mark 7 for 15 minutes.

Maize or Rice Muffins

225g (8 oz) fine maizemeal or
  brown rice flour
15ml (1 tbsp) gluten-free
  baking powder
75g (3 oz) milk-free
  margarine or 50ml
  (2 fl oz) oil of choice

2 eggs
175ml (6 fl oz) goats' milk,
  sheep's milk or soya milk
Grated zest of 1 orange

Stir dry ingedients together and melt the margarine. Whisk eggs until light and fluffy, then gently fold in all the other ingredients. Spoon into 12 greased or oiled muffin cups or bun tins and bake at 200°C, 400°F, Gas Mark 6 for 12–15 minutes.

Herb Muffins

Follow recipe and method for 'Maize or Rice Muffins'. Add finely chopped herbs of choice and omit the orange zest.

Feta Cheese Muffins

Follow recipe and method for 'Maize or Rice Muffins'. Add 115g (4 oz) finely diced Feta Cheese (with or without herbs) and omit the orange zest.

Waffles, Drop Scones and Pancakes

All the recipes in this section are cooked either on a griddle or in a frying pan or waffle maker.

Waffles are an ideal food for the whole family and are invaluable for anyone on a yeast-free diet. They can be made from a wide variety of ingredients and they are both appetizing and nutritious. Any of the following flours or flakes will make good waffles: brown rice flour, chick pea flour, chestnut flour, banana flour, millet flour, rye flour, barley flour, porridge oats, buckwheat flakes or millet flakes.

Waffles (with Egg)

175g (6 oz) flour or flakes of
  choice (see above)
10ml (2 tsp) gluten-free baking
  powder or 2·5ml (½ tsp)
  bicarbonate of soda
1 egg

Pinch of salt
15ml (1 tbsp) oil of choice
150–300ml (¼–½ pt) goats'
  milk, sheep's milk, soya
  milk, 'Nut Milk' (see page
  188) or 'Rice Dream'

Put all ingredients, except the milk, into a bowl. Add some of the milk and beat well, adding more liquid as necessary until the batter is thick but pourable. (The amount of liquid will vary with the type of cereal used.) Leave to stand while the waffle iron is heating up. Adjust the consistency with more liquid, if necessary, as the mixture will thicken as it stands. Use an electric waffle maker or waffle iron which sits on a ring of the hob. Brush liberally with oil all surfaces which will come into contact with the waffles. Heat waffle maker. Pour in sufficient batter just to cover the base of the waffle maker. Waffles freeze well and can be reheated under the grill or in an electric toaster. Serve them for breakfast instead of toast, for hot snacks or at teatime. If you want to serve in the traditional way with ice cream or a sweet sauce for dessert, then add 15ml (1 tbsp) sugar to batter.

Gl Use gluten-free flour or flakes.
Gr Use grain-free flour or flakes and any of the milks except 'Rice Dream'.

C|E / Gl|□ Rice and Soya Waffles

175g (6 oz) brown rice flour
10ml (2 tsp) gluten-free
* baking powder or*
* 2·5ml (½ tsp) bicarbonate*
* of soda*

Pinch of salt
22ml (1½ tbsp) soya oil
90ml (6 tbsp) soya flour
300–350ml (10–12 fl oz)
* soya milk*

Follow the method for 'Waffles (with Egg)' making sure that the plates of the waffle maker are brushed liberally with oil or the waffles will stick.

□|E / Gl|Gr Egg-free Waffles

Follow the recipe and method for 'Waffles (with Egg)' substituting 30ml (2 tbsp) 'Apricot Egg Replacer', 'Date Egg Replacer' (see page 189) or pineapple purée for the egg.

Gl Use gluten-free flour or flakes.
Gr Use grain-free flour or flakes and any of the milks except 'Rice Dream'.

Drop Scones

Drop Scones, or Griddle Scones as they are sometimes called, are made on a hot griddle or a lightly-oiled frying pan.

The batter used is exactly the same as that used for any of the 'Waffles' (see previous two pages). Drop 15–25ml (1–1½ tbsp) onto the hot griddle or lightly oiled frying pan and cook for about three minutes on each side or until golden brown. Serve hot.

See Dietary Notes given for waffle batters.

 # Cheese Drop Scones

The batter used is exactly the same as that used for 'Waffles (with Egg)' or 'Rice and Soya Waffles' (see previous two pages) with the addition of 75g (3 oz) grated Malvern Ewe's cheese or Nanny's Cheddar. Drop 15ml (1 tbsp) batter onto hot griddle or lightly-oiled frying pan and cook for about three minutes on each side or until golden brown. Serve hot.

See Dietary Notes given for waffle batters.

Walnut and Honey Drop Scones

The batter used is exactly the same as that used for 'Waffles (with Egg)' or 'Rice and Soya Waffles' (see previous two pages). Add 50g (2 oz) finely chopped walnuts to the batter and sweeten with 15ml (1 tbsp) honey.

See Dietary Notes given for waffle batters.

Pancakes

The batter used is the same as that used for 'Waffles (with Egg)' (see page 45) or 'Rice and Soya Waffles' (see page 46) but increase the amount of liquid so that the batter flows easily and when poured into the frying pan will quickly coat the base of the pan. Cook until golden brown and then turn and brown the other side. Serve hot with a savoury or sweet filling.

See Dietary Notes given for waffle batters.

 Whole Millet Drop Scones

200g (7 oz) whole millet   *30ml (2 tbsp) water*
2 egg whites   *A good pinch of salt*

Wash the whole millet to remove any dust, place in a bowl and cover with water. Leave to soak overnight. Drain off liquid. Put the soaked and drained cereal into a blender and blend to a smooth paste. Whisk egg whites with 30ml (2 tbsp) water and then stir in the millet to make a thin batter. Season with salt. Drop by spoonfuls onto an oiled and heated frying pan. Brown well on both sides. Serve for breakfast, spread with your favourite topping.

 Millet Fruit Pancakes

175g (6 oz) millet flakes   *2 apples or pears or 175g*
50g (2 oz) milk-free   *(6 oz) pumpkin*
* margarine*   *30ml (2 tbsp) water*
Pinch of cinnamon

Rub flakes and margarine together in a bowl. Add cinnamon. Grate fruit of choice and add to mixture in bowl together with the water and mix well to a soft dough. Leave to stand for 10 minutes. Divide dough into 4 portions and mould into 1·25cm (½") thick cakes. Heat oil in frying pan and cook pancakes gently and evenly on medium heat until golden brown, then turn and cook other side.

Potato Griddle Scones

1 egg, beaten   *450g (1 lb) mashed potato*
A little oil of choice   *A little potato flour*

Add beaten egg and a little oil to the mashed potato. Mix well and then mix in a little potato flour to stiffen the mixture. Form into round cakes with the hands and cook on a hot griddle or frying pan until golden brown on each side.

Biscuits, Savoury and Sweet

▦ Rye Flatbreads

225g (8 oz) rye flour
10ml (2 tsp) gluten-free baking
  powder or 2·5ml (½ tsp)
  bicarbonate of soda

60ml (4 tbsp) oil of
  choice
90ml (6 tbsp) water
Pinch of salt

Sieve flour, baking powder or bicarbonate of soda together, and then add the rest of the ingredients and work to a soft dough. Press into a swiss roll tin. Flatten top with a rolling pin. Make furrows with a fork and cut into 12 oblong shapes. Bake at 180°C, 350°F, Gas Mark 4 for 20–22 minutes or until just golden. Transfer to a wire rack to cool.

Barley Flatbreads

Follow recipe and method for 'Rye Flatbreads', substituting barley flour for rye flour.

 # Amaranth Crispbread

*225g (8 oz) amaranth seeds
  or toasted amaranth flour
10ml (2 tsp) gluten-free
  baking powder or 2·5ml
  (½ tsp) bicabonate of soda*

*Pinch of salt
45ml (3 tbsp) olive oil
60ml (4 tbsp) cold water*

If using amaranth seed, grind into as fine a flour as possible in a blender or coffee grinder. Place flour in a mixing bowl. Stir in the baking powder or bicarbonate of soda, salt and oil and mix well. Finally, add the water and mix until well blended. Press into a swiss roll tin. Flatten top with a rolling pin. Make furrows with a fork and cut into 12 crispbreads. Bake at 180°C, 350°F, Gas Mark 4 for 20 minutes. Cool slightly and then carefully remove crispbreads with a palette knife and place on a wire rack until completely cold.

 # Tapioca Crispbread

*115g (4 oz) milk-free
  margarine or vegetable
  fat
45ml (3 tbsp) water
Pinch of salt*

*225g (8 oz) tapioca flour
10ml (2 tsp) gluten-free
  baking powder or 2·5ml
  (½ tsp) bicarbonate
  of soda*

Place margarine or fat, water and salt together with one third of the flour in a mixing bowl and cream with a fork until just mixed. Sieve remaining flour and baking powder or bicarbonate of soda together and add to the mixture. Knead very thoroughly until smooth. Roll out the dough thinly on a lightly-floured surface. Cut into squares and place on a greased baking sheet. Bake at 180°C, 350°F, Gas Mark 4 for approx. 25 minutes.

Sago Crispbread

115g (4 oz) milk-free
  margarine or vegetable
  fat
45ml (3 tbsp) water
Pinch of salt

250g (9 oz) sago flour
10ml (2 tsp) gluten-free
  baking powder or 2·5ml
  (½ tsp) bicarbonate
  of soda

Follow method and baking instructions for 'Tapioca Crispbread'.

 ## Arrowroot Crispbread

Follow recipe and method for 'Tapioca Crispbread', substituting arrowroot for tapioca flour.

 ## Rice and Buckwheat Crispbread

175g (6 oz) brown rice flour
50g (2 oz) buckwheat flour
Water to mix

30ml (2 tbsp) milk-free
  margarine or oil of choice

Mix all ingredients together using just enough water to make a dough. Roll out thinly on a surface dusted with flour. Cut into oblong biscuits and bake at 220°C, 425°F, Gas Mark 7 for 8–10 minutes. Put on a wire rack to cool and store in an airtight tin.

 ## Scottish Oatcakes

225g (8 oz) medium oatmeal
Pinch of bicarbonate of soda
90ml (6 tbsp) boiling water

15ml (1 tbsp) oil of choice
Pinch of salt (optional)

Place oatmeal in a large mixing bowl and stir in sieved bicarbonate of soda very well to ensure even distribution. Make a well in the centre of the oatmeal. Add the boiling water and the oil to the oatmeal and mix thoroughly to a stiff dough. Roll out thinly on a surface dusted with oatmeal. Cut into rounds using a plain cutter or upturned cup. Place on a greased baking tray and bake at 180°C, 350°F, Gas Mark 4 for 25 minutes. Do not allow to brown.

Breakfast Biscuits

115g (4 oz) barley flour
40g (1½ oz) potato flour
2·5ml (½ tsp) gluten-free
  baking powder or pinch
  of bicarbonate of soda
Pinch of salt
15g (½ oz) medium oatmeal

40g (1½ oz) milk-free
  margarine
40g (1½ oz) demerara
  sugar, ground or
  20g (¾ oz) fructose
45ml (3 tbsp) goats' milk,
  sheep's milk or soya milk

Sieve together flour, baking powder or bicarbonate of soda and salt into a large bowl and add the oatmeal. Rub in margarine, then add sugar or fructose. Mix to a stiff dough with milk. Turn out onto a lightly barley-floured surface and knead well. Roll out thinly and cut into rounds with a 6·5cm (2½") biscuit cutter. Transfer to a greased baking tray and prick well. Bake at 190°C, 375°F, Gas Mark 5 for 15–20 minutes or until light brown. Transfer to wire rack to cool. Store in an airtight tin.

Buckwheat Breakfast Biscuits

75g (3 oz) milk-free margarine
60ml (4 tbsp) water
225g (8 oz) buckwheat flour

2·5ml (½ tsp) bicarbonate
  of soda
Pinch of salt

Put fat, water and half the buckwheat flour in a bowl and cream together. Mix bicarbonate of soda and salt with the rest of the flour, add to the mixture and work to a soft dough. Roll out on a surface dusted with buckwheat flour and cut out with a 6·5cm (2½") plain cutter. Place on a baking tray. Prick all over with a fork and bake at 180°C, 350°F, Gas Mark 4 for 20 minutes. Put on a wire rack to cool and store in an airtight tin.

Chestnut Breakfast Biscuits

Follow recipe and method for 'Buckwheat Breakfast Biscuits', substituting chestnut flour for buckwheat flour.

Barley and Walnut Cookies

*65g (2½ oz) milk-free
  margarine
50g (2 oz) demerara sugar,
  ground or 35g (1¼ oz)
  fructose*

*50g (2 oz) walnuts, finely
  chopped
115g (4 oz) barley flour
10ml (2 tsp) instant chicory
15ml (1 tbsp) water*

Cream margarine and sugar or fructose until light and fluffy, and add walnuts. Stir in sieved flour and instant chicory. Add water and mix. Take spoonfuls of the mixture and roll into balls. Place onto a greased baking tray, spacing well apart, and flatten with the palm or a potato masher. Bake at 190°C, 375°F, Gas Mark 5 for 15–20 minutes. Allow to cool slightly on baking tray and then transfer to a wire rack until cold. Store in an airtight tin.

Digestive Biscuits

*100g (3½ oz) rye flour
Pinch of salt
Pinch of bicarbonate of soda
15g (½ oz) medium oatmeal
40g (1½ oz) milk-free margarine*

*25g (1 oz) sugar or 15g
  (½ oz) fructose
45ml (3 tbsp) goats' milk,
  sheep's milk or
  soya milk*

Sieve together flour, salt and bicarbonate of soda into a large bowl, and add oatmeal. Rub in margarine and add sugar or fructose. Mix to a stiff dough with milk. Turn onto a lightly-floured surface and knead well. Roll out thinly. Cut into rounds with a 6·5cm (2½") biscuit cutter. Transfer to a greased baking tray and prick well. Bake at 190°C, 375°F, Gas Mark 5 for 12–15 minutes. Transfer to a wire rack to cool. Store in an airtight tin.

Brown Rice Digestive Biscuits

115g (4 oz) brown rice flour
Pinch of salt
2·5ml (½ tsp) gluten-free
  baking powder or a pinch
  of bicarbonate of soda

40g (1½ oz) milk-free
  margarine
25g (1 oz) sugar or 15g
  (½ oz) fructose
45ml (3 tbsp) goats' milk,
  sheep's milk or soya milk

Follow method and baking instructions for 'Digestive Biscuits'.

 # Teatime Biscuits

75g (3 oz) chick pea flour
  or barley flour
50g (2 oz) brown rice flour
  or potato flour
25g (1 oz) soya flour

50g (2 oz) milk-free
  margarine
50g (2 oz) sugar or 25g
  (1 oz) fructose
10–20ml (2–4 tsp) water

Put flours and margarine into a bowl and rub in well. Stir in sugar or fructose and add water, a little at a time, to form a dough. Knead until the mixture is smooth and then roll out with a little extra flour. Cut into rounds with a pastry cutter or upturned cup, transfer to a baking tray and prick all over with a fork. Bake at 160ºC, 325ºF, Gas Mark 3 for 10–12 minutes. Carefully remove biscuits from tray while still warm and leave on a wire rack to cool. Store in an airtight tin.

Gl Use chick pea flour.
Gr Use chick pea flour and potato flour.

 # Ginger Nuts

65g (2½ oz) milk-free
  margarine
75g (3 oz) demerara sugar
60ml (4 tbsp) clear honey
  or maple syrup
225g (8 oz) brown rice flour
  or chick pea flour

2·5ml (½ tsp) mixed spice
7·5ml (1½ tsp) ground
  ginger
5ml (1 tsp) bicarbonate
  of soda
15ml (1 tbsp) warm water

Put margarine, sugar and honey or syrup into a pan and melt over very low heat. Sieve flour, spice and ginger into a large bowl. Add melted mixture and bicarbonate of soda mixed with warm water. Mix well and shape into approximately 24 small balls. Put onto greased baking trays, well apart to allow them to spread. Flatten tops with a potato masher. Bake at 160°C, 325°F, Gas Mark 3 for 15 minutes. Leave on trays for 1–2 minutes to set before transferring to a wire rack to cool. Store in an airtight tin.

Gr Use chick pea flour.

Arrowroot and Coconut Biscuits

115g (4 oz) unsulphured
  desiccated coconut
115g (4 oz) arrowroot
10ml (2 tsp) gluten-free baking
  powder or 2·5ml (½ tsp)
  bicarbonate of soda

25g (1 oz) fructose
50g (2 oz) milk-free
  margarine
20ml (4 tsp) water to mix

Put all dry ingredients into a mixing bowl. Rub in the margarine and then add the water. Knead to a soft dough. Roll out on a surface dusted with arrowroot and cut out with a fluted biscuit cutter. Bake at 180°C, 350°F, Gas Mark 4 for 12–15 minutes or until light golden in colour. Leave on tray to partially cool before transferring to a wire rack.

Buckwheat Flapjacks

75g (3 oz) milk-free
  margarine
75g (3 oz) demerara sugar
10ml (2 tsp) black treacle

115g (4 oz) buckwheat
  flakes
Pinch of salt

Melt margarine, sugar and treacle in a saucepan but do not allow it to boil. Add buckwheat flakes and salt and stir well. Press into a shallow oblong tin and bake at 180°C, 350°F, Gas Mark 4 for 20–22 minutes. After removing from the oven leave to set for a few minutes. Cut into fingers while still warm and transfer to a wire rack until completely cold.

Buckwheat and Walnut Biscuits

115g (4 oz) buckwheat flakes　　*60ml (4 tbsp) oil of choice*
30ml (2 tbsp) muscovado sugar　*1 egg, beaten*
50g (2 oz) walnuts, ground

Mix buckwheat flakes, sugar, ground walnuts, oil and beaten egg in a bowl. Place mixture in an oiled oblong tin 23x18cm (9x7"). Smooth top with back of a spoon. Bake at 180°C, 350°F, Gas Mark 4 for 20–22 minutes. Cut into squares and cool on wire rack.

Millet and Hazelnut Biscuits

Follow recipe and method for 'Buckwheat and Walnut Biscuits' substituting millet flakes for buckwheat flakes and ground hazelnuts for ground walnuts.

Almond Pyramids

50g (2 oz) milk-free magarine　*75g (3 oz) potato flour or*
30ml (2 tbsp) clear honey　　　*brown rice flour*
*　maple syrup or rice syrup*　　*Pinch of salt*
50g (2 oz) ground almonds　　*1 egg, beaten*

Beat the margarine and honey or syrup to a cream. Add the ground almonds, flour and salt. Add the beaten egg and mix to a stiff paste. Place in small mounds on an oiled baking sheet and shape into pyramids with a fork. Bake at 180°C, 350°F, Gas Mark 4 for about 20 minutes.

Gr Use potato flour.

Banana Cookies

75g (3 oz) milk-free margarine
50g (2 oz) demerara sugar
50g (2 oz) dried banana,
    chopped

115g (4 oz) banana flour
45ml (3 tbsp) goats' milk,
    sheep's milk or
    soya milk

Put all ingredients into a mixing bowl and beat well. The dough should be very stiff. Roll out on a banana-floured surface and cut into biscuits. Bake at 180°C, 350°F, Gas Mark 4 for 15–20 minutes.

 # Chocolate or Carob Biscuits

115g (4 oz) milk-free
    margarine
115g (4 oz) sugar
    or 50g (2 oz) fructose

1 egg, beaten
250g (9 oz) brown rice flour
25g (1 oz) cocoa powder
    or carob powder

Cream together margarine and sugar or fructose until light and fluffy. Beat in egg gradually. Sieve together flour and cocoa or carob and stir into mixture. Knead lightly on a surface dusted with flour. Roll out thinly and cut into rounds with a 5–6·5cm (2–2½") biscuit cutter. Place on a greased baking tray, leaving room to spread and bake at 160°C, 325°F, Gas Mark 3 for about 20 minutes. Allow to cool slightly before transferring to a wire rack to cool completely. Sandwich together in pairs with 'Chocolate or Carob Filling' (see page 82).

 # Finger Biscuits

225g (8 oz) millet flakes or
    buckwheat flakes
30ml (2 tbsp) oil of choice
15ml (1 tbsp) maple syrup,
    date syrup or molasses

50g (2 oz) dates, finely
    chopped
5ml (1 tsp) ground ginger
2 eggs
Pinch of salt

Put all ingredients into a mixing bowl and beat well. Place in an oiled 18cm (7") square tin and bake at 190°C, 375°F, Gas Mark 5 for approx. 20 minutes. Cool slightly, then cut into fingers while still in the tin. Turn out when cold.

 Use buckwheat flakes.

Gluten-free Florentines

75g (3 oz) milk-free margarine
115g (4 oz) demerara sugar
115g (4 oz) walnuts, chopped
15ml (1 tbsp) brown rice flour

50g (2 oz) flaked hazelnuts
　or flaked almonds
50g (2 oz) natural sultanas
　or natural raisins

Melt the margarine and sugar together in a saucepan over gentle heat. Add the remaining ingredients all at once and stir well to mix. Line baking sheets with non-stick paper and drop in mounds, using a spoon, spacing well apart on the prepared sheets. Press into neat shapes. Bake at 180°C, 350°F, Gas Mark 4 for 12–15 minutes, until golden. Leave on paper until cold and then remove carefully. Coat with 'Carob Icing' (see page 83), if desired.

Potato Shortbread

115g (4 oz) milk-free
　margarine
50g (2 oz) sugar

175g (6 oz) potato flour
75g (3 oz) ground almonds
　or ground cashews

Beat margarine until soft and creamy. Add other ingredients and work until a ball of dough is formed. Put into a greased 18–20cm (7–8") round sandwich tin and press down evenly. Prick all over and bake at 180°C, 350°F, Gas Mark 4 for 35–40 minutes or until lightly golden brown. Cut into 8 wedges.

Rice Shortbread

115g (4 oz) milk-free
　margarine

50g (2 oz) sugar
175g (6 oz) brown rice flour

Cream margarine and sugar and then work in the flour. Knead until the mixture forms a ball of dough and leaves the sides of the bowl clean. Press evenly into a 18–20cm (7–8") sandwich tin and prick all over. Bake at 160°C, 325°F, Gas Mark 3 for 40 minutes or until lightly golden. Allow to cool a little in the tin and then cut into 8 wedges. Transfer to a wire rack until cold.

⬜E̲/G̲l̲G̲r̲ **Tapioca Shortbread**

115g (4 oz) milk-free   *150g (5 oz) tapioca flour*
 margarine   *50g (2 oz) sugar*

Cream all ingredients together and then work until it forms a ball of dough and leaves the sides of the bowl clean. Put into a greased 18–20cm (7–8") sandwich tin and press down evenly. Prick all over and bake at 160°C, 325°F, Gas Mark 3 for 50 minutes. Allow to cool in tin a little and then cut into 8 wedges. Transfer to a wire rack until cold.

⬜E̲/G̲l̲G̲r̲ **Sago Shortbread**

115g (4 oz) milk-free   *225g (8 oz) sago flour*
 margarine   *50g (2 oz) sugar*

Follow method and baking instructions for 'Tapioca Shortbread' using an 20–23cm (8–9") tin.

Cakes, Fillings and Frostings

Tapioca Viennese Fancies

115g (4 oz) tapioca flour
115g (4 oz) milk-free margarine

50g (2 oz) sugar
A little jam

Beat all ingredients except jam together until creamy. Transfer mixture to a piping bag fitted with a large star nozzle. Pipe into bun tins lined with paper cake cases. Start with a little mixture in the centre at the bottom and then pipe two rows in a spiral to leave a hollow in the middle. Bake at 160°C, 325°F, Gas Mark 3 for 50 minutes. Cool on wire rack. When completely cold fill the centres with jam. Dust with icing sugar, if desired.

Coconut Rocks

30ml (2 tbsp) milk-free
  margarine
45ml (3 tbsp) clear honey
  or maple syrup

75ml (5 tbsp) potato flour
45ml (3 tbsp) unsulphured
  desiccated coconut
1 egg, beaten

Beat the margarine together with the honey or syrup. Add the flour and coconut gradually, then the egg, still beating the mixture. Drop spoonfuls onto an oiled baking tray and bake at 220°C, 425°F, Gas Mark 7 for about 8 minutes.

Coconut Macaroons

2 egg whites
115g (4 oz) demerara sugar,
  ground or castor sugar

100g (3½ oz) unsulphured
  desiccated coconut

Whisk the egg whites very stiffly, then fold in the sugar and coconut and mix well. Line a baking sheet with rice paper and drop spoonfuls onto the rice paper, well apart to allow them to spread. Bake at 150°C, 300°F, Gas Mark 2 for 20–25 minutes. Remove from tray and trim off excess rice paper.

Belgian Biscuit Cake

Any of the plain sweet biscuits or shortbreads appearing in this book on pages 53–60 would be suitable for this recipe.

25g (1 oz) milk-free
  margarine
15ml (1 tbsp) maple syrup
  date syrup or rice syrup
65g (2½ oz) 'Green and
  Black's Organic Dark
  Chocolate' or 'Plamil
  Carob Confection'

115g (4 oz) 'Sweet Biscuits'
  or 'Shortbread'
25g (1 oz) natural sultanas
15g (½ oz) stem ginger,
  finely chopped
Rum or orange liqueur
  (optional)

Put margarine, syrup and chocolate or carob in a bowl and melt over a pan of hot water. Place the biscuits in a plastic bag and crush with a rolling pin. Add the crumbs and the rest of the ingredients to the bowl and stir well until the crumbs are completely coated with the mixture. A little rum or orange liqueur may be added, if desired. Pat into a small tin and leave to set. Store in the refrigerator until required. Cut into small wedges and serve as an after-dinner treat.

Gl Use gluten-free biscuits.
Gr Use grain-free biscuits, maple syrup or date syrup.

Coconut Fingers

175g (6 oz) brown rice flour
5ml (1 tsp) bicarbonate
of soda
15g (½ oz) sesame seeds
40g (1½ oz) unsulphured
desiccated coconut
45ml (3 tbsp) oil of choice

Pinch of salt
300ml (½ pt) goats' milk,
sheep's milk, coconut
milk or soya milk
1 egg or 15g (½ oz) 'Cirrus
Whole Egg Replacer' and
45ml (3 tbsp) water

For cake made with egg:
Put all ingredients together into a large bowl and whisk well.
For cake made with whole egg replacer:
Put the egg replacer and water into a bowl and whisk until frothy. Put rest of ingredients into a separate bowl, add 30ml (2 tbsp) of the whisked egg replacer and mix well. Fold in the rest of the whisked egg replacer.
Pour the prepared mixture into an oiled swiss roll tin and bake at 220°C, 425°F, Gas Mark 7 for 15–20 minutes. Allow to cool in the tin and then cut into fingers. Transfer to a wire rack until completely cold.

E Use *'Cirrus Whole Egg Replacer'*.

Millet Rock Cakes

75g (3 oz) millet flour or
    millet flakes
75g (3 oz) brown rice flour
    or chick pea flour
5ml (1 tsp) gluten-free
    baking powder
50g (2 oz) milk-free
    margarine

75g (3 oz) sugar or 40g
    (1½ oz) fructose
Pinch of nutmeg
Pinch of mixed spice
25g (1 oz) natural currants
1 egg
Goats' milk, sheep's milk or
    soya milk to mix

If using millet flakes, place them in a blender and turn into flour.
Mix flours and baking powder together. Rub in milk-free margarine
and add sugar, spice and currants. Mix well. Add egg and a little
milk and mix to a very stiff dough. Place in mounds on a greased
baking sheet and bake at 200°C, 400°F, Gas Mark 6 for 15 minutes.

Chewy Coconut Bars

First Layer:
75g (3 oz) milk-free
    margarine
75g (3 oz) demerara sugar
115g (4 oz) flour of choice

Second Layer:
2 eggs, lightly beaten

A few drops of Bourbon
    vanilla extract
75g (3 oz) unsulphured
    desiccated coconut
75g (3 oz) walnuts, chopped
25g (1 oz) flour of choice
175g (6 oz) demerara sugar
2·5ml (½ tsp) salt

To make first layer:
Beat margarine and sugar together until fluffy and mix in flour.
Put mixture into a greased swiss-roll tin and bake for 10 minutes
at 180°C, 350°F, Gas Mark 4.
To make second layer:
Put all ingredients for second layer into a bowl and mix well.
Spread mixture over part-cooked first layer. Return to the oven
and bake for a further 20 minutes. Cool. Cut into bars and leave
in tin until completely cold.

Gl Use a gluten-free flour of choice.
Gr Use a grain-free flour of choice.

Coconut Brownies

Cake:
50g (2 oz) 'Green and
   Black's Organic Dark
   Chocolate' *or* 'Plamil
   Carob Confection'
65g (2½ oz) milk-free
   margarine
2 eggs
175g (6 oz) sugar
75g (3 oz) brown rice flour
   or banana flour
2·5ml (½ tsp) gluten-free
   baking powder

Pinch of salt
65g (2½ oz) unsulphured
   desiccated coconut

Topping:
15g (½ oz) milk-free
   margarine
15ml (1 tbsp) demerara
   sugar
65g (2½ oz) unsulphured
   desiccated coconut

To make the cake:
Melt chocolate or carob and milk-free margarine in a bowl over a
pan of hot water. Set aside to cool. Beat eggs until fluffy. Gradually
add sugar and beat until well blended. Add melted chocolate or
carob flour, baking powder, salt and coconut. Beat well and spread
into a greased 20cm (8") square tin.

To make the topping:
Melt the margarine and stir in the rest of the sugar and coconut.
Scatter evenly over the cake batter and bake for 30 minutes at
180°C, 350°F, Gas Mark 4. Cool in tin and cut into 16 squares.
Transfer to wire rack until completely cold.

Gr Use banana flour.

Fruit and Lemon Buns

115g (4 oz) brown rice flour
   or banana flour
7·5ml (1½ tsp) gluten-free
   baking powder
2 eggs, beaten
115g (4 oz) sugar or 135g
   (4½ oz) glucose or 65g
   (2½ oz) fructose

5ml (1 tsp) lemon rind,
   grated
115g (4 oz) milk-free
   margarine or 65ml
   (2½ fl oz) oil of choice
30ml (2 tbsp) water
75g (3 oz) natural sultanas

Sieve flour and baking powder together. Add all the rest of the ingredients except the sultanas and beat very well. Stir in sultanas. Put spoonfuls into paper cake cases on a baking tray or into greased bun tins and bake at 200°C, 400°F, Gas Mark 6 for approx. 15 minutes.

Variations:
Natural raisins, chopped dates or figs may be used instead of sultanas.

 Use banana flour.

Millet Buns

115g (4 oz) milk-free
  margarine
115g (4 oz) sugar
115g (4 oz) millet flour
  or millet flakes

2 eggs, beaten
115g (4 oz) natural currants
25g (1 oz) flaked almonds or
  flaked hazelnuts

If using millet flakes, place them in a blender and turn into flour. Cream margarine and sugar until light and fluffy. Fold in beaten eggs and millet flour a little at a time and finally stir in the fruit and nuts. Put spoonfuls into paper cake cases on a baking tray or into greased bun tins. Bake at 200°C, 400°F, Gas Mark 6 for 15–20 minutes.

Potato and Buckwheat Buns

50g (2 oz) potato flour
7·5ml (1½ tsp) gluten-free
  baking powder
50g (2 oz) buckwheat flakes
30ml (2 tbsp) water
2 eggs, beaten

115g (4 oz) sugar or 135g
  (4½ oz) glucose or 65g
  (2½ oz) fructose
115g (4 oz) milk-free
  margarine or 65ml
  (2½ fl oz) oil of choice

Sieve potato flour and baking powder together and stir in buckwheat flakes. Place all the rest of the ingredients in the mixing bowl and beat very well with a wooden spoon. Put spoonfuls into paper cake cases on a baking tray or into greased bun tins. Bake at 200°C, 400°F, Gas Mark 6 for approx. 15 minutes.

⊞E̲ GI̲Gr̲ Eggless Sponge Cakes

115g (4 oz) milk-free margarine
115g (4 oz) sugar or 50g (2 oz) fructose
25g (1 oz) 'Cirrus Whole Egg Replacer'

90ml (6 tbsp) water
175g (6 oz) brown rice flour or banana flour
7·5ml (1½ tsp) gluten-free baking powder

Cream margarine and sugar or fructose until pale and fluffy. Put whole egg replacer and water into a bowl and whisk well. Sieve flour and baking powder together, and gently fold flour and a little whisked egg replacer into creamed mixture. Finally fold in the rest of the whisked egg replacer. Put spoonfuls into paper cake cases on a baking tray and bake at 200°C, 400°F, Gas Mark 6 for 15–20 minutes.

Gr̲ Use banana flour.

⊞E̲ GI̲☐ Eggless Rock Cakes

225g (8 oz) brown rice flour
12·5ml (2½ tsp) gluten-free baking powder
15g (½ oz) 'Cirrus Whole Egg Replacer'
45ml (3 tbsp) water

150g (5 oz) milk-free margarine
150g (5 oz) sugar or 65g (2½ oz) fructose
50g (2 oz) natural raisins
50g (2 oz) natural sultanas
50g (2 oz) natural currants

Sieve flour and baking powder together into a large mixing bowl. Put whole egg replacer and water into a bowl and whisk well. Rub margarine into flour and stir in sugar or fructose. Fold in egg replacer mixture to make a stiff consistency. Gently stir in dried fruit. Put spoonfuls into paper cake cases or greased bun tins and bake at 220°C, 425°F, Gas Mark 7 for about 10–12 minutes.

Sugar-free Carob Butterfly Cakes

1 large carrot
1 large apple or pear
2 eggs
115g (4 oz) brown rice flour,
     barley flour or banana flour
2·5ml (½ tsp) bicarbonate
     of soda
15ml (1 tbsp) carob powder

65ml (2½ fl oz) oil
     of choice

Filling:
75g (3 oz) 'Plamil Carob
     Confection'
150ml (¼ pt) sheep's
     yoghurt or 'Soya Creem'

Peel and dice carrot and apple. Place in a blender or food processor together with the eggs. Run the machine until mixture is smooth and fluffy. Place flour, bicarbonate of soda and carob powder in a large bowl and mix well. Add egg mixture to flour together with the oil and fold in gently with a metal spoon. Spoon mixture into oiled bun tins and bake at 190°C, 375°F, Gas Mark 5 for 15 minutes. Place on a wire rack until cold. Cut off the top of each cake and then cut each top in half. Place a spoonful of the filling on each cake and replace halved tops at an angle to form 'wings'.
To make the filling:
Break up the carob bar into small pieces and gently melt in a bowl over a pan containing boiling water. Remove from the heat and beat in the yoghurt or *'Soya Creem'*. Chill until thickened.

Gl Use brown rice flour or banana flour.
Gr Use banana flour.

Flapplejack

1 large eating apple
30ml (2 tbsp) oil of choice

115g (4 oz) millet flakes
     or buckwheat flakes

Grate apple into a bowl. Add oil and flakes and stir until well mixed. Put into a cake tin which has been brushed with oil. Press down with potato masher. Bake at 180°C, 350°F, Gas Mark 4 for 30 minutes, or more, until cake is firm and dry. Cut into wedges.

Gr Use buckwheat flakes.

Mud Huts

Chocolate or carob sponge cakes with chocolate or carob filling.

*115g (4 oz) milk-free
 margarine or 65ml
 (2½ fl oz) oil of choice
115g (4 oz) sugar or
 135g (4½ oz) glucose
 or 65g (2½ oz) fructose
2 eggs, beaten*

*115g (4 oz) brown rice
 flour
15ml (1 tbsp) cocoa
 powder or carob powder
7·5ml (1½ tsp) gluten-free
 baking powder
30ml (2 tbsp) water
A little jam (optional)*

For cakes made with margarine:
Put margarine and sweetener of choice into a large bowl and
cream together until fluffy. Add beaten egg. Sieve together flour,
baking powder and cocoa or carob. Beat into creamed mixture
together with water.
For cakes made with oil:
Sieve together flour, baking powder and cocoa or carob into a
large bowl. Add all the rest of the ingredients and beat very well.

Put spoonfuls into paper cake cases on a baking tray or into greased
bun tins and bake at 200°C, 400°F, Gas Mark 6 for approx. 15
minutes. Put on a wire rack to cool. Cut a small lid out of the top
of each cake. Put a tiny blob of jam in each hollow (optional).
Cover jam with a spoonful of 'Chocolate or Carob Filling' (see
page 82) and replace the lid.

Pumpkin and Coconut Cake

*75g (3 oz) pumpkin, grated
2·5ml (½ tsp) mixed spice*

*2 eggs
75g (3 oz) unsulphured
 desiccated coconut*

Grease a Pyrex pie plate or similar ovenproof dish. Put the grated
pumpkin into a bowl, add the mixed spice and mix thoroughly
until the mixed spice is evenly incorporated. Stir in the coconut.
Whisk the eggs until fluffy and then fold into the pumpkin mixture.

Place in the prepared dish and smooth top with a palette knife. Bake at 180ºC, 350ºF, Gas Mark 4 for 25–30 minutes, until top is golden.

⊟E̲|G̲l̲G̲r̲ Apricot Squares

*115g (4 oz) unsulphured
    dried apricots
150ml (¼ pt) water
115g (4 oz) potato flour
    or tapioca flour
7·5ml (1½ tsp) gluten-free
    baking powder*

*115g (4 oz) porridge oats,
    buckwheat flakes or
    millet flakes
115g (4 oz) milk-free
    margarine
60ml (4 tbsp) maple syrup,
    rice syrup or honey*

Grease a shallow 18cm (7") square tin with milk-free margarine. Place apricots in a pan with the water. Bring to the boil and then simmer gently, stirring occasionally, until all the water has been absorbed and apricots are tender. Beat mixture until smooth and set aside. Sieve flour and baking powder into a bowl and stir in flakes and sugar. Rub in margarine until mixture begins to stick together. Measure syrup or honey carefully and blend into cake mixture. Press half of the cake mixture into base of tin, spread apricots over this and then top with remaining cake mixture. Spread evenly. Bake at 190ºC, 375ºF, Gas Mark 5 for 35–40 minutes, until cake is golden brown. Leave in the tin to become quite cold before cutting into squares.

G̲l̲ Use millet flakes or buckwheat flakes.
G̲r̲ Use buckwheat flakes, maple syrup or honey.

⊟E̲|G̲l̲G̲r̲ Date Squares

Follow recipe and method for 'Apricot Squares' substituting dates for apricots. Date syrup may also be substituted for honey or maple syrup.

See Dietary Notes for 'Apricot Squares'.

Buckwheat Crunchy Topped Squares

Topping:
75g (3 oz) milk-free
  margarine
30ml (2 tbsp) golden syrup
  or maple syrup
50g (2 oz) natural sultanas
  or natural raisins
75g (3 oz) buckwheat flakes
75g (3 oz) unsulphured
  desiccated coconut
50g (2 oz) demerara sugar

Cake:
115g (4 oz) milk-free
  margarine
115g (4 oz) demerara sugar,
  ground
2 eggs or 25g (1 oz) 'Cirrus
  Whole Egg Replacer' and
  90ml (6 tbsp) water
50g (2 oz) potato flour
50g (2 oz) buckwheat flour
7·5ml (1½ tsp) gluten-free
  baking powder

For topping:
Put the margarine and syrup into a saucepan and set over gentle heat until margarine has melted. Stir in rest of ingredients and set aside.

For cake made with egg:
Cream the margarine and sugar until fluffy. Beat the eggs and add with the rest of the ingredients and mix well.

For cake made with whole egg replacer:
Cream the margarine and sugar until fluffy. Put the whole egg replacer into a large bowl together with the water and whisk well. Put the dry ingredients into the creamed mixture together with a spoonful of the whisked egg replacer and mix well. Fold in the rest of the whisked egg replacer.

Spread cake mixture over the base of a greased and lined 23x18cm (9x7") tin, cover with the topping and smooth top with the back of a spoon. Bake at 180°C, 350°F, Gas Mark 4 for 50 minutes or until golden brown.

E Use *'Cirrus Whole Egg Replacer'*.

Millet Crunchy Topped Squares

Topping:
75g (3oz) milk-free
  margarine
30ml (2 tbsp) golden syrup,
  maple syrup or rice syrup
50g (2 oz) natural sultanas
  or natural raisins
75g (3 oz) millet flakes
75g (3 oz) unsulphured
  desiccated coconut
50g (2 oz) demerara sugar

Cake:
115g (4 oz) milk-free
  margarine
115g (4 oz) demerara sugar,
  ground
2 eggs or 25g (1 oz) 'Cirrus
  Whole Egg Replacer' and
  90ml (6 tbsp) water
115g (4 oz) brown rice flour
  or millet flour
7·5ml (1½ tsp) gluten-free
  baking powder

Follow method for 'Buckwheat Crunchy Topped Squares'.

E Use *'Cirrus Whole Egg Replacer'*.

Sugar-free Sponge Cake

115g (4 oz) brown rice flour,
  barley flour, banana flour
  or rye flour
2·5ml (½ tsp) bicarbonate
  of soda

1 large carrot
1 large apple or pear
2 eggs   '
65ml (2½ fl oz) oil
  of choice

Place flour and bicarbonate of soda in a large bowl and mix well.
Peel and dice carrot and apple or pear. Place in a blender or food
processor together with eggs. Run machine until mixture is smooth
and fluffy. Add oil to the flour and then gently fold in the egg
mixture with a metal spoon. Pour mixture into oiled and floured
18cm (7") sandwich tin and bake at 190°C, 375°F, Gas Mark 5 for
20 minutes.

Gl Use brown rice flour or banana flour.
Gr Use banana flour.

Sugar-free Fruit Cake

250g (9 oz) chick pea flour
10ml (2 tsp) bicarbonate
of soda
5ml (1 tsp) cinnamon
5ml (1 tsp) mixed spice
2 medium-sized eating
apples or pears

1 medium-sized carrot
350ml (12 fl oz) water
45ml (3 tbsp) milk-free
margarine
150g (5 oz) natural currants
150g (5 oz) natural sultanas

Mix flour, bicarbonate of soda and spices together in a large bowl. Chop apples or pears and carrot, put into a blender or food processor with the measured water and blend. Add to flour mixture along with other ingredients and beat well with a wooden spoon. Pour mixture into a greased and *unlined* 20cm (8") cake tin and bake in centre of the oven at 190°C, 375°F, Gas Mark 5 for approximately 1 hour. Eat within a week.

Honey and Hazelnut Cake

200ml (7 fl oz) clear
honey
25g (1 oz) milk-free
margarine
175g (6 oz) brown rice
flour or barley flour
Pinch of salt
2·5ml (½ tsp) mixed spice

1 egg
5ml (1 tsp) bicarbonate
of soda
45ml (3 tbsp) goats'
milk, sheep's milk
or soya milk
45ml (3 tbsp) flaked
hazelnuts

Put the honey and margarine in a small pan over low heat until margarine is melted. Remove from the heat and mix. Sieve together the flour, salt, and spices. Add these to the melted mixture with the egg and beat well. Dissolve the bicarbonate of soda in the milk and stir into the cake mixture. Turn into a greased and floured sandwich tin and sprinkle with the flaked hazelnuts. Bake at 180°C, 350°F, Gas Mark 4 for 25–30 minutes. Turn out onto a wire rack to cool.

Gl Use brown rice flour.

⊞ Fudge Cake
Gl Gr

50g (2 oz) 'Green and
  Black's Organic Dark
  Chocolate' *or* 'Plamil
  Carob Confection'
30ml (2 tbsp) water
115g (4 oz) milk-free
  margarine
200g (7 oz) soft brown sugar
A few drops of Bourbon
  vanilla extract
2 eggs
150ml (¼ pt) goats' milk,
  sheep's milk or soya milk
200g (7 oz) brown rice flour
  or banana flour

15ml (3 tsp) gluten-free
  baking powder
Juice of ½ lemon
30ml (2 tbsp) apricot jam

Frosting:
450g (1 lb) demerara sugar
150ml (¼ pt) water
20ml (4 tsp) golden syrup
  or maple syrup
50g (2 oz) milk-free
  margarine
40–50g (1½–2 oz) cocoa
  powder or carob powder

Grease a 18cm (7") round cake tin and line with greased greaseproof paper. Break chocolate or carob bar into small pieces in bowl. Add the water and stand over a pan of gently boiling water stirring occasionally until smooth; remove from heat and allow to cool slightly. Cream the margarine with sugar and vanilla until light and fluffy. Beat in lightly whisked eggs and melted chocolate or carob. Add the lemon juice to the milk. Mix together the flour and baking powder. Add these two mixtures alternately, a little at a time, to the cake mixture, beating after each addition. Turn mixture into prepared tin and smooth over the top. Bake at 180°C, 350°F, Gas Mark 4 for 1–1½ hours or until cake is cooked through. Leave to cool in tin for 10 minutes before turning on to a wire rack. When cold, brush the top of cake with warmed jam and then spread fudge frosting over the top using a palette knife to swirl the frosting.

To prepare Fudge Frosting:
Place sugar, water, syrup, milk-free margarine and cocoa or carob into heavy-based pan. Stir over gentle heat until sugar has dissolved. Bring to 112°C, 234°F on a sugar thermometer, then remove from heat. Cool for 10–15 minutes, then beat with wooden spoon until thick and of spreading consistency. Use at once.

Gr Use banana flour.

Rice Flour Sponge Cake

115g (4 oz) milk-free
  margarine or 65ml
  (2½ fl oz) oil of choice
115g (4 oz) sugar or
  135g (4½ oz) glucose or
  65g (2½ oz) fructose

2 eggs, beaten
115g (4 oz) brown rice flour
7·5ml (1½ tsp) gluten-free
  baking powder
30ml (2 tbsp) water

For cake made with margarine:
Cream margarine and sweetener of choice, and then add eggs. Mix together flour and baking powder and fold into mixture with water.
For cake made with oil:
Sieve flour and baking powder together. Add all the rest of the ingredients and beat very well.
Put into a greased and floured 18–20cm (7–8") sandwich tin and bake at 200°C, 400°F, Gas Mark 6 for 20–22 minutes. Remove from oven and allow to stand for a few minutes and then turn out onto a wire rack to cool.

Banana Flour Sponge Cake

Follow recipe and method for 'Rice Flour Sponge Cake' substituting banana flour for brown rice flour.

Rye Flour Sponge Cake

Follow recipe and method for 'Rice Flour Sponge Cake' substituting rye flour for brown rice flour.

Tropicana Cake

40g (1½ oz) unsulphured
  desiccated coconut
115g (4 oz) milk-free
  margarine
75g (3 oz) demerara sugar
10ml (2 tsp) lemon rind,
  grated
325g (11 oz) banana flour

10ml (2 tsp) gluten-free
  baking powder or 2·5ml
  (½ tsp) bicarbonate of soda
2 eggs or 25g (1 oz) 'Cirrus
  Whole Egg Replacer'
  and 90ml (6 tbsp) water
115ml (4 fl oz) pineapple
  juice or apple juice
3 dried bananas, chopped

Place coconut on a baking tray and toast under the grill. Cream margarine and sugar, add lemon rind and beat well. Add eggs one at a time, beating well after each addition. Sieve together flour and baking powder. Fold into mixture alternately with pineapple or apple juice and toasted coconut. Add chopped dried bananas and mix well. Put mixture into a greased and bottom-lined 1kg (2 lb) loaf tin and bake at 180°C, 350°F, Gas Mark 4 for 1–1¼ hours.
For cake made with whole egg replacer:
Whisk the whole egg replacer with the water and fold into the cake mixture as the final ingredient.

E Use *'Cirrus Whole Egg Replacer'*.

Rich Mocha Cake

Cake:
3 eggs
115g (4 oz) castor sugar
25g (1 oz) brown rice flour
  or chick pea flour
1·25ml (¼ tsp) gluten-free
  baking powder
25g (1 oz) cocoa powder
  or carob powder
5ml (1 tsp) instant chicory
  or instant coffee

Icing and decoration:
115g (4 oz) milk-free
  margarine
175g (6 oz) icing sugar
2·5ml (½ tsp) cocoa powder,
  carob powder, instant
  coffee or instant chicory
50g (2 oz) 'Green & Black's
  Organic Dark Chocolate'
  or 'Plamil Carob
  Confection'

Grease and line two 23cm (9") sandwich tins with greased greaseproof paper. Break the eggs into a mixing bowl over a pan of hot water, add the sugar and whisk for about 8 minutes till thick. Remove the bowl from the heat and continue to whisk till the mixture is cool. Sieve the flour, baking powder, cocoa or carob and the instant chicory or coffee, and fold into the mixture. Divide evenly between the two prepared tins. Bake in the centre of oven at 190°C, 375°F, Gas Mark 5 for about 20 minutes till cooked. Cool in the tins for 5 minutes.

To ice and decorate:
Cream the margarine, gradually beating in the icing sugar which has been sieved with the flavouring of choice. Continue beating until smooth. Stand one cake on the serving plate and spread with half the icing and place second cake on top. Spread remaining icing over the top and rough up the surface with the palette knife. Coarsely grate the chocolate or carob bar over the top and dredge with icing sugar.

Gr Use chick pea flour.

 ## Coconut Cake

160g (5½ oz) milk-free margarine or 80ml (3 fl oz) oil of choice	15ml (3 tsp) gluten-free baking powder
225g (8 oz) demerara sugar	115g (4 oz) unsulphured desiccated coconut
4 eggs	45ml (3 tbsp) goats' milk,
225g (8 oz) brown rice flour or banana flour	sheep's milk, coconut milk or soya milk

Grease and line an 20cm (8") deep cake tin or a 1kg (2 lb) loaf tin.

For cake made with margarine:
Cream together the margarine and sugar until fluffy. Beat the eggs lightly and gradually beat into creamed mixture, alternately with the flour and baking powder. Finally add the coconut and the milk.

For cake made with oil:
Place all ingredients in a bowl and beat very well.
Put into the prepared tin and smooth over the top. Bake at 160°C, 325°F, Gas Mark 3 for 1½ hours.

Gr Use banana flour.

⊞ Barley Parkin

Barley flakes are rather tough and need to be chopped or minced to give this cake the correct texture.

175g (6 oz) barley flakes
50g (2 oz) barley flour
2·5ml (½ tsp) bicarbonate
  of soda
10ml (2 tsp) ground ginger
1 egg or 15g (½ oz) 'Cirrus
  Whole Egg Replacer' and
  45ml (3 tbsp) water

75g (3 oz) muscovado sugar
75g (3 oz) milk-free
  margarine or 50ml
  (2 fl oz) oil of choice
175g (6 oz) black treacle
30ml (2 tbsp) goats' milk,
  sheep's milk or soya milk

Lightly chop the barley flakes in a blender or food processor or put through a mincer. Sieve the flour, bicarbonate of soda and ginger. Stir in the minced barley flakes, beaten egg and sugar. Warm the milk-free margarine (if using) and the treacle and milk and stir into the mixture. Beat in the oil (if using). Beat well and pour into greased or oiled and bottom-lined 20cm (8") square tin and bake for about 40 minutes at 180°C, 350°F, Gas Mark 4. Keep for a few days before use to allow the cake to mature.

For cake made with whole egg replacer:
Whisk the whole egg replacer with the water and fold into the cake mixture as the last ingredient.

E Use *'Cirrus Whole Egg Replacer'*.

⊞ Walnut Cake

175g (6 oz) milk-free
  margarine
175g (6 oz) demerara sugar
  or 100g (3½ oz) fructose
3 eggs and 15ml (1 tbsp)
  water or 40g (1½ oz)
  'Cirrus Whole Egg Replacer'
  and 225ml (8 fl oz) water

225g (8 oz) barley flour or
  brown rice flour
15ml (1 tbsp) gluten-free
  baking powder
15ml (1 tbsp) instant chicory
  or instant coffee
50g (2 oz) walnuts,
  chopped

Cream margarine and sugar or fructose until light and fluffy.

For cake made with eggs:
Beat eggs and add a little at a time, beating well after each addition. Add water and beat again. Then fold in sieved dry ingredients and chopped walnuts.

For cake made with whole egg replacer:
Put whole egg replacer in a large bowl. Add 225ml (8 fl oz) water and whisk well. Sieve dry ingredients and fold both mixtures into creamed margarine a little at a time until well mixed. Add chopped walnuts and stir gently into cake mixture.

Grease a 1kg (2 lb) loaf tin and line base with greaseproof paper. Place mixture in prepared tin, level top with the back of a spoon and bake at 160°C, 325°F, Gas Mark 3 for 1¼–1½ hours. Leave to cool in tin for about 10 minutes before turning out onto a wire rack to cool completely. Cut cake in half and spread with 'Fructose Cream Filling' or 'Vanilla Cream Filling' (see page 81) and then put back together again.

E Use *'Cirrus Whole Egg Replacer'*.
Gl Use brown rice flour.

C Gl Gr Candida Cake

225g (8 oz) maizemeal, brown rice flour, millet flour or banana flour
5ml (1 tsp) bicarbonate of soda
5ml (1 tsp) ground ginger
15ml (1 tbsp) sesame seeds (optional)

Pinch of salt
300ml (½ pt) goats' milk, sheep's milk or soya milk
60ml (4 tbsp) olive oil
2 eggs
75g (3 oz) unsulphured desiccated coconut

Brush a 20–23cm (8–9") tin with oil. Mix together flour of choice, bicarbonate of soda, ginger and salt. Blend or whisk in all the rest of the ingredients well. Pour into prepared tin and bake at 220°C, 425°F, Gas Mark 7 for 20–25 minutes. Cut into squares while still in tin and then transfer to a rack to cool.

Gr Use banana flour.

⊞⊞ Honey Tea Loaf
GlGr

75g (3 oz) natural raisins
75g (3 oz) natural sultanas
60ml (4 tbsp) clear honey
150ml (¼ pt) cold rooibosch
  tea
1 egg, beaten

5ml (1 tsp) bicarbonate
  of soda
30ml (2 tbsp) water
225g (8 oz) brown rice flour,
  banana flour or barley flour
Honey to glaze

Put fruit and measured honey into a basin and cover with cold rooibosch tea. Leave to soak overnight. Stir in egg and beat well. Dissolve the bicarbonate of soda with the water and add to mixture together with the flour of choice and mix thoroughly. Turn into a greased and lined 500g (1 lb) loaf tin and bake at 180°C, 350°F, Gas Mark 4 for 1–1¼ hours until firm and browned. Leave to cool in tin for 10 minutes, then turn onto a wire rack until cold. Brush top with honey to give a sticky glaze.

This loaf will improve in flavour and become more moist if stored in an airtight tin for a few days before use.

Gl Use brown rice flour or banana flour.
Gr Use banana flour or 115g (4 oz) potato flour and 115g (4 oz) buckwheat flour.

⊞⊞ Gingerbread
GlGr

115g (4 oz) milk-free
  margarine or 65ml
  (2½ fl oz) oil of choice
115g (4 oz) black treacle
300ml (½ pt) goats' milk,
  sheep's milk or soya milk
275g (10 oz) brown rice
  flour, chick pea flour or
  banana flour
15ml (3 tsp) gluten-free
  baking powder

5ml (1 tsp) ground ginger
2·5ml (½ tsp) mixed spice
Pinch of salt
225g (8 oz) raw cane
  sugar
1 egg, beaten or 15g (½ oz)
  'Cirrus Whole Egg
  Replacer' and 45ml
  (3 tbsp) water
5ml (1 tsp) bicabonate of
  soda

For cake made with egg:
Place margarine (if using), treacle and all except 60ml (4 tbsp) of the milk in a pan. Set over gentle heat and melt but do not boil.

Sieve flour, baking powder, ginger, mixed spice and salt into a bowl. Stir in the sugar. Pour melted ingredients into a well in centre of the flour. Add the oil (if using), beaten egg and the bicarbonate of soda which has been dissolved in the reserved 60ml (4 tbsp) of milk. Beat well until smooth.

For cake made with whole egg replacer:
Put the whole egg replacer into a large bowl. Add 45ml (3 tbsp) water and whisk well. Fold the whisked whole egg replacer into the cake mixture as the last ingredient.

Pour into a greased and lined 20–23cm (8–9") square tin. Bake at 180°C, 350°F, Gas Mark 4 for ½ hour, then reduce heat to 160°C, 325°F, Gas Mark 3 for a further ¾ hour. Cover with a sheet of greaseproof paper during the later stages of baking to prevent the top from burning. Best made a few days before required and stored in an airtight tin.

E Use *'Cirrus Whole Egg Replacer'*.
Gr Use banana flour or chick pea flour.

⬚⬚E Fructose Cream Filling
   GlGr

Grind some fructose to a fine powder using a blender, coffee grinder or food processor. Put 30ml (2 tbsp) milk-free margarine into a bowl and add a little ground fructose. Beat well and add more ground fructose, beating well after each addition, until required consistency is achieved.

(Store surplus ground fructose in a screw-top jar.)

⬚⬚E Vanilla Cream Filling
   GlGr

Put 30ml (2 tbsp) milk-free margarine into a bowl. Add either icing sugar or ground fructose (see previous recipe). Add a little of the chosen sweetener at a time, beating well after each addition until the required consistency is achieved. Add a very little Bourbon vanilla extract to taste and beat well. Check for flavour.

Chocolate or Carob Filling

For alternative filling see 'Rich Chocolate Sauce' and 'Rich Carob Sauce' on pages 121 and 122.

15ml (1 tbsp) cocoa powder
*   *or carob powder*
45ml (3 tbsp) icing sugar,
*   *glucose or finely ground*
*   *fructose (see 'Fructose Cream*
*   *Filling')*
15ml (1 tbsp) milk-free
*   *margarine or oil of choice*

15ml (1 tbsp) goats' milk,
*   *sheep's milk or*
*   *soya milk*
15–60ml (1–4 tbsp)
*   *powdered goats' milk,*
*   *powdered sheep's milk*
*   *or powdered soya milk*

Sieve cocoa or carob powder into a bowl. Add oil or margarine and beat. Add 15ml (1 tbsp) of sweetener of choice and milk. Beat again and then add rest of sweetener and sufficient powdered milk to obtain required consistency. The amount of powdered milk required will vary depending upon whether margarine or oil has been used.

Chocolate or Carob and Hazelnut Filling

15–30ml (1–2 tbsp) 'Meridian
*   *Hazelnut Butter'*

5–10ml (1–2 tsp) cocoa
*   *powder or carob powder*

Place hazelnut butter in a bowl and add sieved cocoa or carob powder. Work together with a fork until well mixed. If mixture is too stiff then blend in a little milk-free margarine.

Carob Frosting

75g (3 oz) 'Plamil Carob
*   *Confection'*
30ml (2 tbsp) water

30ml (1 oz) milk-free
*   *margarine*

Break the carob bar into small pieces. Place the water and the carob in a saucepan over a gentle heat, and stir until carob has melted. Remove from heat and beat in the margarine. Allow to cool slightly and then spread over the top of the cake.

☐E GI Gr Chocolate Frosting

Use recipe and method for 'Carob Frosting' substituting *'Green and Black's Organic Dark Chocolate'* for carob.

CE GI Gr Carob Icing

Gives a harder coating than the frosting and so is more suitable for biscuits, florentines and pastries.

75g (3 oz) 'Plamil Carob Confection'

25g (1 oz) milk-free margarine

Break carob bar into small pieces. Melt carob and margarine together over a gentle heat and beat until smooth. Use immediately. To ice biscuits: Draw the biscuit over the surface of the icing. Leave on a wire rack until set and then store in a tin.

☐E GI Gr Soya Marzipan

150g (5 oz) soft light brown sugar
50g (2 oz) soya flour
25g (1 oz) milk-free margarine

2·5ml (½ tsp) natural almond essence
7·5ml (½ tbsp) water

Put all dry ingredients into a large mixing bowl and rub in the margarine until well incorporated. Add the almond essence and the water and mix until pliable, adding a little more water if necessary.

Pastries and Cold Desserts

C E Gl Gr Sago Shortcrust Pastry

250g (9 oz) sago flour
115g (4 oz) milk-free
* margarine*

Pinch of salt
30ml (2 tbsp) water

Sieve flour and salt into mixing bowl. Rub in the margarine until the mixture resembles fine breadcrumbs. Add sufficient water to mix until it clings together. If too sticky add a little more flour. Roll out pastry on sago flour and use as required. Bake at 200°C, 400°F, Gas Mark 6 until crisp or according to recipe used.

Rice Pastry

50g (2 oz) milk-free
margarine
115g (4 oz) brown rice flour

75g (3 oz) eating apple,
grated
Pinch of salt

Put all ingredients into a bowl and blend together with a fork. Knead until it forms a large ball of dough. Roll out on brown rice flour. Bake at 200°C, 400°F, Gas Mark 6 until crisp or use according to recipe.

 ## Pastry made with Oil

75ml (5 tbsp) oil of choice
45ml (3 tbsp) cold water
225g (8 oz) rye flour, buckwheat
flour, brown rice flour or
chick pea flour

5ml (1 tsp) gluten-free
baking powder or 1·25ml
(¼ tsp) bicarbonate of soda
Pinch of salt

Whisk oil and water together. Put all ingredients into a large mixing bowl and work together to form a soft dough.

As the dough is more difficult to handle than pastry made with a fat, put it in the centre of the plate or flan dish and work it with the hands to cover the entire surface. Bake in the usual way.

Gl Use brown rice flour, chick pea flour or buckwheat flour.
Gr Use chick pea flour or buckwheat flour.

 ## Buckwheat and Potato Pastry

50g (2 oz) milk-free
margarine
50g (2 oz) buckwheat flour

50g (2 oz) potato flour
1 eating apple, grated
Pinch of salt

Put all ingredients into a bowl and blend with a fork. Knead until it forms a large ball of dough. Roll out or press into tin with the fingers. Bake at 180°C, 350°F, Gas Mark 4 for 15–20 minutes for individual tarts or 25–35 minutes for flans and plate pies. The temperature is a little lower than usual as this pastry tends to burn easily.

Chick Pea and Potato Pastry

Follow recipe and method for 'Buckwheat and Potato Pastry' substituting chick pea flour for buckwheat flour.

Rice and Potato Pastry

75g (3 oz) brown rice flour
40g (1½ oz) soya flour
75g (3 oz) potato flour
Water to mix

50g (2 oz) milk-free
*   margarine*
30ml (2 tbsp) almonds
*   or cashews, ground*

Put all ingredients into a bowl and blend with a fork, adding sufficient water to mix. Knead well. Roll out on brown rice flour, or for a plate tart, put the whole ball of pastry in the centre of the plate and press it flat, gradually working towards the edge of the plate. Bake at 200°C, 400°F, Gas Mark 6 until crisp or according to recipe used.

Rye Pastry

200g (7 oz) rye flour
2·5ml (½ tsp) gluten-free
*   baking powder or pinch of*
*   bicarbonate of soda*

Pinch of salt
75ml (5 tbsp) water
60ml (4 tbsp) olive oil

Put all ingredients into a large mixing bowl and work together to form a soft dough. As the dough is difficult to handle, put the ball of dough in the centre of the plate or flan dish and work to fit with the hands. Bake in the usual way.

Date Flan

Line an 18–20cm (7–8") flan tin with pastry of choice (see pages 84–86).

Filling:
115g (4 oz) dates   30ml (2 tbsp) water

Chop the dates finely and put into a saucepan with the water. Simmer gently, stirring with a wooden spoon, until all liquid is absorbed and the mixture forms a smooth paste. Put into uncooked pastry case, smooth over the top with the back of a spoon. Decorate the top with leftover pastry cut into attractive shapes with mini-cutters, if desired. Bake at 190°C, 375°F, Gas Mark 5 for 35 minutes. Serve with 'Coconut Cream' (see page 188).

Gl Use gluten-free pastry of choice.
Gr Use grain-free pastry of choice.

Apricot Flan

Line an 18–20cm (7–8") flan tin with pastry of choice (see pages 84–86).

Filling:
115g (4 oz) unsulphured   30ml (2 tbsp) water
    dried apricots   Sweeten to taste

Follow method for 'Date Flan'. (If Hunza apricots are being used: Put apricots into a saucepan with just enough water to cover. Simmer gently until soft and then remove the stones. Drain off excess liquid and mash to a smooth paste.)

Gl Use gluten-free pastry of choice.
Gr Use grain-free pastry of choice.

Bakewell Tart

Line an 18–20cm (7–8") flan tin with pastry of choice (see pages 84-86).

Filling:

50g (2 oz) milk-free
   margarine
50g (2 oz) demerara sugar,
   ground or castor sugar

1 egg
50g (2 oz) ground almonds
Raspberry jam

Spread some raspberry jam in the base of the uncooked pastry case. Cream together margarine and sugar until light and fluffy. Beat egg and fold into mixture together with the ground almonds. Put into pastry case and smooth over the top. Bake at 200°C, 400°F, Gas Mark 6 for 25–30 minutes.

Gl Use gluten-free pastry of choice.
Gr Use grain-free pastry of choice.

Peacheesy Flan

Line an 18–20cm (7–8") fluted flan ring with pastry of choice (see pages 84-86) and place on a baking tray.

Filling:

2 large peaches
15ml (1 tbsp) cornflour,
   tapioca flour or arrowroot
5ml (1 tsp) mixed spice
A few drops of Bourbon
   vanilla extract

Topping:

1 egg
65g (2½ oz) castor sugar
10ml (2 tsp) lemon juice
30ml (2 tbsp) peach syrup
15ml (1 tbsp) goats' milk
   or sheep's milk
40g (1½ oz) soft goats'
   cheese, soft sheep's
   cheese or 'Curd Cheese'
   (see page 185)

Peel and slice peaches and poach lightly in a little sweetened water. Drain, reserving syrup. Put cornflour, tapioca flour or arrowroot into a bowl with mixed spice and vanilla and mix together. Add drained peaches and stir. Place peach mixture in flan case. Place egg, sugar, lemon juice and peach syrup in a small pan. Cook over a low heat, stirring until mixture thickens, but do not boil. Remove from the heat; beat in milk and soft or curd cheese. Pour over peach mixture. Bake in centre of oven at 200°C, 400°F, Gas Mark 6 for 10 minutes and then reduce temperature to 180°C, 350°F, Gas Mark 4 and cook for a further 30–35 minutes, until topping is golden brown. Serve hot or cold.

Gl Use gluten-free pastry of choice.
Gr Use grain-free pastry of choice and arrowroot or tapioca flour.

Yoghurt and Apricot Flan

Line a 20–23cm (8–9") fluted flan ring with pastry of choice (see pages 84-86) and place on a baking tray.

Filling:
225g (8 oz) unsulphured
  dried apricots, soaked
15ml (3 tsp) gelatine
  or 7·5ml (1½ tsp)
  agar agar
30ml (2 tbsp) hot water

300ml (½ pt) natural goats'
  yoghurt or sheep's yoghurt
1 egg white
3 fresh apricots or drained
  canned apricots in juice
Honey to taste, if desired

Bake the pastry case 'blind' for 15 minutes at 190°C, 375°F, Gas Mark 5. Remove the baking beans and bake, uncovered, for a further 5 minutes. Cook the soaked apricots for 20 minutes in the soaking water. Purée the fruit. Dissolve the gelatine or agar agar in the hot water, according to the manufacturer's instructions. Stir in the apricot purée. Fold in the yoghurt. Check for flavour and sweeten with honey, if desired. Whisk egg whites and fold into apricot mixture. Pour into the baked and cooled flan case and leave to set. Halve and stone the fresh apricots or use 6 tinned apricot halves. Place the apricot halves at equal distances around edge of flan.

Gl Use gluten-free pastry of choice.
Gr Use grain-free pastry of choice.

Baked Cheesecake

1 batch of pastry of choice, using 170g (6 oz) flour (see pages 84-86).

Filling:
450g (1 lb) goats' or sheep's   *115g (4 oz) sugar*
  Curd Cheese (see page 185) *25g (1 oz) natural sultanas*
1 egg white, beaten   *Goats' milk or sheep's milk*
          to glaze

Line the bottom of an 18cm (7") square tin with two thirds of the pastry. Roll out rest of pastry and cut into 23cm (9") strips about 0·75cm (¼") wide. Place all ingredients for filling in a bowl and mix well. Turn into pastry-lined tin, and arrange pastry strips in a lattice pattern. Brush pastry lattice with goats' milk or sheep's milk. Bake for 45–50 minutes at 190°C, 375°F, Gas Mark 5. Cool for 30 minutes in tin, then when really set take out.
Cut into squares and serve.

Gl Use gluten-free pastry of choice.
Gr Use grain-free pastry of choice.

Cheesecake

Any of the plain sweet biscuits or shortbreads appearing in this book on pages 53-60 would be suitable for this recipe.

115g (4 oz) 'Sweet Biscuits'   *50g (2 oz) castor sugar*
  or 'Shortbread'   *or 25g (1 oz) fructose*
50g (2 oz) milk-free   *175g (6 oz) soft goats' cheese,*
  margarine   *soft sheep's cheese or 'Curd*
10ml (2 tsp) gelatine   *Cheese' (see page 185)*
  or 5ml (1 tsp) agar agar *80ml (3 fl oz) goats' milk*
25ml (5 tsp) very hot water   *or sheep's milk*
1 large egg yolk   *1 large lemon*

Put the biscuits into a large plastic bag and crush with a rolling pin. Melt margarine in a saucepan and stir in the biscuit crumbs.

Lightly grease a loose-bottomed cake tin. Spoon biscuit mixture into cake tin and press down well with a potato masher. Chill in refrigerator for two hours. Dissolve the gelatine or agar agar in the hot water, according to the manufacturers' instructions, and leave to cool but not set. Put egg yolk, sugar or fructose, cheese and milk into blender and mix for 1 minute. Squeeze the juice from half the lemon and add 45ml (3 tbsp) to the blender along with the cooled gelatine or agar agar and mix again. Pour this mixture onto the set biscuit base in the cake tin and return to the refrigerator for a further two hours.* Just before serving, thinly slice the remaining half lemon and cut each slice in half. Arrange around outside edge of top of cheesecake.

Slices of Kiwi Fruit make a very attractive alternative decoration.

To remove from tin: Place tin on top of a container such as a tin of treacle and very gently draw down the sides of the cake tin. Transfer to serving plate using a palette knife to ease the cheesecake from the cake tin base.

Gl Use gluten-free biscuits or shortbread of choice.
Gr Use grain-free biscuits or shortbread of choice.

Fruit Topped Cheesecake

Follow recipe and method for 'Cheesecake' as far as the *. These are usually topped with cherries or pineapple but any fruit is suitable (tinned, bottled, frozen or fresh). Before removing the cheesecake from the tin decorate the top with fruit of choice. Blend 10ml (2 tsp) cornflour, arrowroot or tapioca flour with 75ml (5 tbsp) juice in a saucepan. Bring to the boil, then stir over a low heat for 1 minute. Spoon over fruit and leave to set. Remove from tin as described at end of previous recipe.

Gl Use gluten-free biscuits or shortbread of choice.
Gr Use grain-free biscuits or shortbread of choice and arrowroot or tapioca flour for topping.

Cassata Cheese Pears

4 large Comice or William
*   pears*
150g (5 oz) soft goats' cheese,
*   soft sheep's cheese or 'Curd*
*   Cheese' (see page 185)*

Juice of 1 lemon
25g (1 oz) natural currants
25g (1 oz) natural sultanas
Parsley

Cut a small slice off the top of each pear. Remove 5 thin strips of peel, forming ridges from top to bottom and brush with lemon juice. Carefully remove cores, and brush inside with lemon juice. Combine cheese and dried fruit and pile into hollow centres and in a small mound on top of each pear. Stand pears on individual dishes and top each with a tiny sprig of parsley. Serve as a starter or a dessert.

 # Hawaiian Pineapple

1 small ripe pineapple
A few strawberries or
*   raspberries to decorate*

225g (½ lb) soft goats' cheese,
*   soft sheep's cheese or 'Curd*
*   Cheese' (see page 185)*

Cut pineapple into quarters lengthways, scoop out flesh and chop. Place cheese in a bowl and stir in chopped pineapple. Pile into pineapple 'shells' and decorate each with strawberries or raspberries. Place on a serving dish and keep cool until ready to serve.

 # Orange Jelly

20ml (4 tsp) gelatine or
*   10ml (2 tsp) agar agar*
150ml (¼ pt) hot water
300ml (½ pt) orange juice

Sweetener of choice
45ml (3 tbsp) lemon juice
150ml (¼ pt) cold water

Add gelatine or agar agar to hot water and dissolve according to the manufacturers' instructions. Allow to cool. Mix with the rest of the ingredients and place in a rinsed mould. Leave in refrigerator to set.

Fruit Jelly

*20ml (4 tsp) gelatine or
    10ml (2 tsp) agar agar
150ml (¼ pt) hot water*

*450ml (¾ pt) pure
    unsweetened fruit juice*

Add gelatine or agar agar to hot water and dissolve according to
the manufacturers' instructions. Allow to cool. Mix with the juice
and place in a rinsed mould. Leave to set in refrigerator.

 Mandarin Orange Jelly

*20ml (4 tsp) gelatine or
    10ml (2 tsp) agar agar*

*1 tin mandarin orange
    segments in natural juice*

Dissolve the gelatine or agar agar in a little hot water according
to the manufacturers' instructions. Leave to cool. Meanwhile,
empty the contents of the tin into a blender and blend until
smooth. Pour both mixtures into a measuring jug and top up to ½
litre (1 pt) with cold water. Pour into a bowl or jelly mould and
leave in the refrigerator to set.
Other tasty fruits in natural juice are also good for making jelly in
this way.

 Milk Jelly

*20ml (4 tsp) gelatine or
    10ml (2 tsp) agar agar
45ml (3 tbsp) hot water
Sweetener of choice*

*450ml (¾ pt) goats' milk,
    sheep's milk, soya milk,
    coconut milk or 'Nut
    Milk' (see page 188)*

Dissolve gelatine or agar agar in hot water according to
manufacturers' instructions, and allow to cool. Add sweetener
and gradually stir in milk. Pour into mould or serving dish and
leave in refrigerator to set. Serve with fruit.

Fruit Mousse

20ml (4 tsp) gelatine or
   10ml (2 tsp) agar agar
45ml (3 tbsp) hot water
2 eggs

Small pinch of salt
575ml (1 pt) fruit purée
Sweetener of choice

Dissolve gelatine or agar agar in hot water according to manufacturers' instructions. Beat egg yolks thoroughly. Sweeten fruit purée according to taste and add to the egg yolks. Place bowl over a pan of hot water and stir until quite hot. Leave to cool. Add dissolved gelatine or agar agar. Add salt to egg whites and beat until stiff. Fold into mixture and pour into serving bowl. Leave in refrigerator to set.

 # Carob or Chocolate Dessert

20ml (4 tsp) gelatine or
   10ml (2 tsp) agar agar
500–575ml (¾–1 pt) goats'
   milk, sheep's milk or
   soya milk

15ml (1 tbsp) carob powder
   or cocoa powder
A few drops of Bourbon
   vanilla extract
30ml (2 tbsp) maple syrup

Dissolve the gelatine or agar agar in a little hot water according to the manufacturers' instructions. When dissolved mix with sufficient milk to make up to ½ litre (1 pt). Pour into blender along with the rest of the ingredients and blend until smooth. Pour into a dish or mould and chill until set.

 # Vanilla Delight

2 eggs
30ml (2 tbsp) sugar or honey
Pinch of salt
450ml (¾ pt) goats' milk
   or sheep's milk

Piece of vanilla pod or a few
   drops of Bourbon vanilla
   extract
20ml (4 tsp) gelatine or
   10ml (2 tsp) agar agar
45ml (3 tbsp) hot water

Beat egg yolk lightly and set aside. Add sugar or honey and salt to milk along with the vanilla pod, if using. Heat until nearly boiling, pour over beaten eggs and return to heat. Cook until the mixture thickens and breaks into curds and whey. (If separation is not required, do not boil the custard. Heat gently until the mixture thickens). Remove the vanilla pod. Dissolve the gelatine or agar agar in the hot water, according to the manufacturers' instructions, and add carefully to mixture. Beat egg whites until stiff and fold into the mixture. Flavour with Bourbon vanilla extract, if using. Place in a mould and leave to set in refrigerator.

Apricot Cream

225g (8 oz) unsulphured
  dried apricots
65ml (2½ fl oz) water
Sweetener of choice

45ml (3 tbsp) cornflour or
  arrowroot
575ml (1 pt) goats' milk
  or sheep's milk
3 egg yolks

Simmer apricots with water until soft and smooth, then sweeten according to taste and rub through a sieve. Mix flour with a little milk. Bring rest of milk to the boil. Pour over blended flour and return to pan to thicken, stirring well. Add sweetened purée whisked with the egg yolks. Continue cooking gently until thick, but do not allow to boil. Pour into serving dish and leave to set.

Gr Use arrowroot.

Gooseberry Fool

225g (8 oz) gooseberries
65ml (2½ fl oz) water
Sweetener of choice
45ml (3 tbsp) cornflour or
  arrowroot

½ litre (1 pt) goats' milk
  or sheep's milk
3 egg yolks
Fresh fruit for decoration

Simmer the fruit with the water and sweetener of choice until very soft and smooth. Sieve or purée the cooked fruit. Mix cornflour or arrowroot with a little milk. Bring rest of the milk to the boil. Pour over mixed flour, stirring well, and return to pan to thicken. Add sweetened purée whisked with egg yolks. Continue cooking gently until thick, but do not allow to boil as mixture will curdle. Pour into rinsed mould or individual dishes. Before serving decorate with reserved fruit.

Gr Use arrowroot.

Blackcurrant Fool

Follow recipe and method for 'Gooseberry Fool' substituting blackcurrants for gooseberries.

Raspberry Fool

Follow recipe and method for 'Gooseberry Fool' substituting raspberries for gooseberries.

Strawberry Fool

Follow recipe and method for 'Gooseberry Fool' substituting strawberries for gooseberries.

Blackberry Fool

Follow recipe and method for 'Gooseberry Fool' substituting blackberries for gooseberries.

Blueberry Fool

Follow recipe and method for 'Gooseberry Fool' substituting blueberries for gooseberries.

Vanilla Ice Cream

575ml (1 pt) goats' milk
  or sheep's milk
Piece of vanilla pod or a few
  drops of Bourbon vanilla
  extract to taste
2 eggs

5ml (1 tsp) gelatine or
  2·5ml (½ tsp) agar agar
30ml (2 tbsp) hot water
75g (3 oz) sugar or
  50g (2 oz) fructose

Measure half of the milk. Beat eggs with a little of this first half. Boil the remainder of this half of the milk with the vanilla pod, if using. Pour over eggs and stir well. Strain into saucepan and cook gently (do not allow to boil), stirring continuously until custard coats back of spoon. Leave to cool. Dissolve gelatine or agar agar in hot water, according to the manufacturers' instructions, and add to custard with the sugar or fructose and Bourbon vanilla extract, if using. Stir in the second half of the milk. Pour into shallow container and place in the freezer. When the mixture is firm round the edges, turn into a chilled bowl and beat thoroughly. Return to container and freeze till firm.

Chocolate Ice Cream

Follow recipe and method for 'Vanilla Ice Cream' omitting the vanilla and substituting 100g (3½ oz) *'Green and Black's Organic Dark Chocolate'*. Place in a pan with a little of the second half of the milk and heat gently until the chocolate has melted. Set aside to cool before adding with the rest of the second half of the milk to the prepared custard.

Carob Ice Cream

Follow recipe and method for 'Vanilla Ice Cream' omitting the vanilla and substituting 100g (3½ oz) *'Plamil Carob Confection'*. Place in a pan with a little of the second half of the milk and heat gently until the carob has melted. Set aside to cool before adding with the rest of the second half of the milk to the prepared custard.

Coffee Ice Cream

Follow recipe and method for 'Vanilla Ice Cream' omitting the vanilla and substituting 15ml (1 tbsp) instant coffee. Add to a little of the second half of the milk and heat gently to disperse.

Chicory Ice Cream

Follow recipe and method for 'Vanilla Ice Cream' omitting the vanilla and substituting 30ml (2 tbsp) *'Prewett's Instant Chicory'*. Add to a little of the second half of the milk and heat gently to disperse.

Fruit Ice Cream

Follow recipe and method for 'Vanilla Ice Cream' omitting the vanilla and substituting 300ml (½ pt) fruit purée instead of the second half of the milk. Add extra sugar or fructose to taste.

Tutti Frutti Ice Cream

Follow recipe and method for 'Vanilla Ice Cream' adding 115g (4 oz) dried fruit and nuts to the mixture before the final freezing.

Rose Ice Cream

Follow recipe and method for 'Vanilla Ice Cream' omitting the vanilla and substituting a little distilled rose water to taste when adding the sweetener.

Honey Ice Cream

Follow recipe and method for 'Vanilla Ice Cream' omitting the vanilla and using honey instead of sugar.

 # Raspberry Sorbet

225g (8 oz) raspberries
300ml (½ pt) goats' yoghurt
   or sheep's yoghurt
15ml (1 tbsp) lemon juice

10ml (2 tsp) gelatine or
   5ml (1 tsp) agar agar
Sweetener of choice
2 egg whites

Mash and sieve the raspberries. Mix purée with yoghurt and lemon juice. Dissolve the gelatine or agar agar in a little hot water, according to the manufacturers' instructions. Stir into purée and sweeten to taste. Whisk the egg whites until stiff and carefully fold into fruit mixture. Pour into containers and freeze.
To serve: Thaw for a short while in the fridge to bring out the flavour.

 # Chocolate or Carob Blancmange

45ml (3 tbsp) cornflour or
   arrowroot
15ml (1 tbsp) cocoa powder
   or carob powder

15–30ml (1–2 tsp) sugar or
   7–15ml (½–1 tsp) fructose
575ml (1 pt) goats' milk,
   sheep's milk or soya milk

Use the smaller amount of sweetener if using carob powder and the larger amount of sweetener if using cocoa.
Mix dry ingredients with a little of the cold milk. Bring the rest of the milk to the boil and pour over the mixture, stirring well. Return to heat to thicken and then simmer for 2–3 minutes. Pour into serving dish and leave to cool. Put into the refrigerator to set.

Gr Use arrowroot.

Arrowroot Blancmange

120ml (8 tbsp) arrowroot   *850ml (1½ pt) goats' milk,*
20ml (4 tsp) sugar or   *sheep's milk or soya milk*
* 10ml (2 tsp) fructose*   *A few drops of Bourbon*
                                                  vanilla extract

Put arrowroot and sweetener of choice into a bowl or jug; add a
little of the measured milk and mix well. Meanwhile, put rest of
the milk on to boil. Pour boiling milk over arrowroot, stirring all
the time. Return to pan and heat, stirring all the time, until thick.
Simmer gently for 2–3 minutes. Remove from heat and stir in
vanilla extract. Pour into a serving bowl and chill until set. Serve
with stewed fruit or fresh fruit salad.

 ## Grape Dessert

½ litre (1 pt) grape juice   *Fresh grapes*
90ml (6 tbsp) arrowroot

Skin, deseed and chop some fresh grapes. Put arrowroot into a
bowl and add a little of the measured grape juice. Put the rest of
the grape juice in a saucepan and bring to the boil. Pour over the
mixed arrowroot and stir well. Return to pan and heat, stirring
all the time, until thick. Simmer for 2–3 minutes. Remove from
the heat, cool and stir in the chopped grapes. Taste to see if it
needs sweetening. Pour into individual sundae dishes and leave
to set. When ready to serve decorate with a few halved and
deseeded grapes.

Chocolate or Carob Millet Crème

55g (2¼ oz) millet flakes
50g (2 oz) natural raisins
30ml (2 tbsp) sugar or
  honey

30ml (2 tbsp) cocoa powder
  or carob powder
575ml (1 pt) goats' milk,
  sheep's milk or soya milk

Pour milk into non-stick pan. Add millet flakes, sweetener of choice and raisins. Mix cocoa or carob into a paste with a little of the milk and then add it to saucepan. Bring the mixture to the boil, stirring, and cook gently for 6–10 minutes until creamy. Remove from heat and cool. Pour into individual glasses or dishes and leave to set.

Pear and Millet Dessert

225g (8 oz) whole millet
50g (2 oz) demerara sugar
575ml (1 pt) goats' milk,
  sheep's milk or soya milk

2 large pears
Almonds or hazelnuts, flaked
'Chocolate or Carob Sauce'
  (see page 121)

Combine the millet, sugar and milk in a pan. Bring to the boil and simmer gently for 30 minutes. Cool the mixture a little and then divide between 4 sundae dishes. Leave until completely cold. Just before serving, peel, core and halve the pears putting half into each dish. Cover with 'Chocolate or Carob Sauce' and sprinkle with flaked nuts.

Rhubarb and Ginger Whip

575g (1¼ lb) rhubarb
30ml (2 tbsp) clear honey
  or maple syrup
1 piece of stem or crystallised
  ginger

225ml (8 fl oz) sheep's
  yoghurt or 'Soya Creem'
25g (1 oz) flaked almonds

Trim rhubarb, removing any coarse stringy pieces. Cut into small pieces and cook gently with a little water until soft. Sweeten to taste. Finely chop the ginger and stir into the rhubarb. Allow to cool. Gently fold in the yoghurt or *'Soya Creem'* and divide between four serving dishes. Sprinkle flaked almonds over the top.

Creamy Fruit Condé

Make a 450g (1 lb) rice, tapioca or sago pudding using goats', sheep's, soya or 'Nut Milk' (see page 188) and leave until cold.

20ml (4 tsp) gelatine or   *450g (1 lb) fresh tasty fruit*
  10ml (2 tsp) agar agar   *such as raspberries*

Dissolve gelatine or agar agar in a little hot water, according to the manufacturers' instructions. When dissolved, make up to 450ml (¾ pt) with cold water. Add a little lemon juice to sharpen the flavour, if desired. Put half the fruit in a bowl and reserve the rest for decoration. Either chop or slightly mash the fruit, according to type. Mix the cold pudding, fruit and 300ml (½ pt) of the cooled jelly and pour into 4 individual sundae dishes. Place in the refrigerator until just set. Arrange remainder of the fruit on top and spoon the remainder of jelly over the fruit to glaze. Place in refrigerator until set.

Gr Use tapioca or sago pudding.

Creamy Fig Condé

Follow recipe and method for 'Creamy Fruit Condé' using 425g (15 oz) tinned green figs or poached fresh figs together with 75g (3 oz) natural sultanas.

Gr Use tapioca or sago pudding.

⊞ Honey Trifle
Gl Gr

Sponge mixture:
50g (2 oz) honey
3 eggs
Pinch of salt
65g (2½ oz) brown rice
  flour, banana flour
  or barley flour

Filling & topping:
350–450g (¾–1 lb) fruit
  in natural juice (tinned)
½ litre (1 pt) Fruit Jelly
  (see page 93)

45–60ml (3–4 tbsp)
  Martini Rosso or Stone's
  Ginger Wine (optional)
45ml (3 tbsp) cornflour or
  arrowroot
½ litre (1 pt) goats' milk,
  sheep's milk or soya milk
3 egg yolks
Honey to taste
225g (8oz) sheep's yoghurt
  or 'Soya Creem'
Good handful of flaked
  almonds

To make the sponge cake:
Oil and bottom-line a sandwich tin with greaseproof paper. Put the honey and eggs into a bowl and place over a pan of simmering water. Whisk until mixture is pale, thick and leaves a trail. Remove from heat and continue to whisk until mixture is too thick to whisk comfortably. Stir salt into sieved flour and gently fold into mixture using a metal spoon. Pour into tin and bake at 180°C, 350°F, Gas Mark 4 for 18–20 minutes. Cool on a wire rack.

To assemble the trifle:
Cut the cake into pieces and place in bottom of a large serving bowl. Drain fruit and mix a little juice with wine or just use fruit juice. Spoon liquid over sponge pieces but do not saturate. Cover with fruit. Using the rest of the juice, make up jelly and leave until cool. Pour very gently over fruit and sponge. Place in the fridge to set for a few hours. Make custard by blending cornflour or arrowroot with a little of the milk. Bring the rest of the milk to the boil. Pour over mixed flour, stirring well and return to the pan to thicken. Whisk egg yolks with a little honey and add to pan, stirring well. Continue cooking very gently until thick but do not boil. Remove from heat and allow to cool. Stir every so often to prevent a skin forming. When nearly cold pour over the jelly and return to the fridge to set. Place yoghurt or 'Soya Creem' in a small bowl and mix with 5–10 ml (1–2 tsp) honey to taste. Spread over custard and sprinkle flaked almonds over the top. Chill.

Gl Use brown rice flour or banana flour.
Gr Use banana flour and arrowroot.

Prune and Tofu Dessert

115g (4 oz) unsorbated   *30ml (2 tbsp) clear honey,*
  prunes   *maple syrup or date syrup*
225g (8 oz) tofu

Soak the prunes overnight. Drain and place in a saucepan with sufficient fresh water to cover. Simmer for 10–15 minutes until really tender. Remove any stones. Drain again (reserving the liquor) and place in a blender or food processor together with the tofu and sweetener of choice. Blend. Add just enough of the cooking liquor to make a thick but soft purée and reblend. Pour into 4 sundae glasses and chill until ready to serve.

Apricot and Tofu Dessert

Follow recipe and method for 'Prune and Tofu Dessert' substituting unsulphured dried apricots for prunes.

Hot Puddings and Sweet Sauces

 ## Pineapple Upside-down Pudding

200g (7 oz) milk-free
  margarine
185g (6½ oz) demerara
  sugar
425g (15 oz) can pineapple
  rings in natural juice
30ml (2 tbsp) carob powder

30ml (2 tbsp) hot water
3 eggs
175g (6 oz) brown rice flour
10ml (2 tsp) gluten-free
  baking powder or 2·5ml
  (½ tsp) bicarbonate of soda

Grease a 1 litre (2 pt) pudding basin with 25g (1 oz) milk-free margarine and then sprinkle with 15g (½ oz) demerara sugar. Drain the pineapple rings and arrange around the sides and base of basin. Cream together the remaining milk-free margarine and sugar. Blend the carob and hot water, cool and beat gradually into creamed mixture. Beat in the eggs. Sieve the flour and baking powder together and fold into mixture. Carefully spoon over the arranged pineapple. Cover with greased greaseproof paper, pleated in the centre, and tie tightly with string and make a string handle. Steam over boiling water for 2 hours or bake uncovered at 180°C, 350°F, Gas Mark 4 for 45–55 minutes. Serve with custard or pineapple sauce made by thickening the reserved pineapple juice with arrowroot or cornflour.

Fruit and Nut Roly-Poly Pudding

Filling:
450g (1 lb) fruit of choice
Sugar to taste
75g (3 oz) nuts of choice,
    roughly chopped and
    toasted

Sponge mixture:
2 eggs
50g (2 oz) demerara sugar,
    ground or castor sugar
75g (3 oz) nuts of choice,
    ground
25g (1 oz) brown rice flour,
    banana flour or
    chick pea flour

Make a fruit purée first by simmering fruit of choice until soft. Leave to cool and then rub through a sieve. Sweeten to taste. Brush a swiss-roll tin with oil and line with oiled greaseproof paper. Whisk the eggs and sugar in a bowl over a pan of simmering water until pale and thick and the mixture leaves a trail. Remove from the heat and cool a little. Fold in the ground nuts and flour. Pour the mixture into the prepared tin. Bake at 220°C, 425°F, Gas Mark 7 for 12 minutes only. Sprinkle some sugar onto a sheet of greaseproof paper and turn the sponge out onto this. Quickly spread some of the fruit purée onto the sponge and sprinkle with the chopped nuts. Roll up the sponge using the paper to help. Serve immediately with the rest of the fruit purée served in a sauce boat.

Suggested fruit and nut combinations:
Apricot, plums or cherries with almonds.
Raspberries or loganberries with hazelnuts.
Gooseberries or blackcurrants with cashews.

Gr Use banana flour or chick pea flour.

Fat-free Mini Sponges with Fruit Coulis

Sponge:
3 eggs
75g (3 oz) demerara sugar,
   ground or castor sugar
65g (2½ oz) brown rice flour,
   banana flour or
   chick pea flour

Fruit Coulis:
175g (6 oz) raspberries
   or blueberries
10ml (2 tsp) icing sugar
5ml (1 tsp) lemon juice

Brush a 12 hole bun tin or fancy moulds with oil of choice. Sprinkle the inside of each tin with extra sugar, shaking away any excess. Whisk eggs and sugar in a bowl over a pan of simmering water until pale and thick and mixture leaves a trail. Remove the bowl from the heat and continue whisking gently until the mixture cools a little. Gently fold in the flour. Spoon the mixture into the prepared tins, filling them approximately two-thirds full. Sprinkle tops with a pinch of sugar. Bake at 180°C, 350°F, Gas Mark 4 for 12–15 minutes, when the puddings should be firm to the touch. Serve hot or cold with a fruit coulis.
To make Fruit Coulis:
Purée the raspberries or blueberries with the icing sugar and lemon juice in a blender or food processor. Sieve to remove the seeds.

Gr Use banana flour or chick pea flour.

Sugar-free Cabinet Puddings

115g (4 oz) brown rice flour,
  banana flour or barley flour
2·5ml (½ tsp) bicarbonate
  of soda
1 large carrot
1 large eating apple

2 eggs
60ml (4 tbsp) oil
  of choice
60ml (4 tbsp) blackberry
  and apple or blackcurrant
  sugar-free spread

Place flour and bicarbonate of soda in a large bowl and mix well. Peel and dice carrot and apple. Place in a blender or food processor together with the eggs. Run machine until mixture is smooth and fluffy. Add egg mixture to the flour together with the oil and gently fold in with a metal spoon. Divide the sugar-free spread between 8 oiled dariole moulds or 4 oiled ramekin dishes. Cover with the sponge mixture and bake at 190°C, 375°F, Gas Mark 5 for 20 minutes.

Gl Use brown rice flour or banana flour.
Gr Use banana flour.

Sticky Date Puddings

Follow recipe and method for 'Sugar-free Cabinet Puddings' adding 50g (2 oz) dates and substituting 60ml (4 tbsp) date syrup for sugar-free fruit spread. Chop the dates finely and mix with the flour before making the sponge mixture. Place 15ml (1 tbsp) date syrup in the base of each ramekin and cover with the sponge mixture ensuring that the syrup is sealed in.
Serve with 'Coconut Cream' (see page 188).

Gl Use brown rice flour or banana flour.
Gr Use banana flour.

Sugar-free Carob Puddings

115g (4 oz) brown rice flour,
  banana flour or barley flour
2·5ml (½ tsp) bicarbonate
  of soda
15ml (1 tbsp) carob powder

2 large carrots
2 eggs
60ml (4 tbsp) oil
  of choice

Sieve flour, bicarbonate of soda and carob powder into a large bowl. Peel and chop the carrots and place in a blender or food processor together with the eggs. Run machine until mixture is smooth and fluffy. Add egg mixture to the flour together with the oil and gently fold in with a metal spoon. Divide the mixture between 8 oiled dariole moulds or 4 oiled ramekin dishes and bake at 190ºC, 375ºF, Gas Mark 5 for 20 minutes.
Serve with 'Rich Carob Sauce' (see page 122).

C Serve with 'Coconut Cream' (see page 188).
Gl Use brown rice flour or banana flour.
Gr Use banana flour.

Sugar-free Almond and Mandarin Puddings

Use mandarins, clementines or satsumas for these VERY tangy puddings.

3 mandarin oranges
3 eggs, separated
225g (8 oz) carrot
50g (2 oz) brown rice flour

1·25ml (¼ tsp) bicarbonate
  of soda
115g (4 oz) ground almonds
225g (8 oz) sheep's yoghurt
  or 'Soya Creem'

Grease four ramekins and line bases with greaseproof paper discs. Grate the zest from two of the oranges and squeeze the juice from one of these. Peel the other two oranges and remove the membrane from each segment: reserve for decoration. Place egg yolks and 15ml (1 tbsp) orange juice in a bowl and whisk until thick and leaves a trail. Peel and finely grate carrot and gently fold into egg yolk mixture together with 30ml (2 tbsp) of the orange zest. Mix flour and bicarbonate of soda together and then very gently fold this into the mixture followed by the ground almonds. Whisk egg whites until stiff but not dry and fold gently and gradually into mixture. Spoon carefully into prepared ramekin dishes, smooth tops and bake at 170ºC, 325ºF, Gas Mark 3 for approximately 45 minutes. Leave to cool for a few minutes. Run knife around ramekins to loosen the sides of the puddings, turn out onto individual serving plates and remove paper discs. Serve puddings with yoghurt or *'Soya Creem'* and decorate with reserved segments.

Sugar-free Eve's Puddings

115g (4 oz) brown rice flour,
*   banana flour or barley flour*
2·5ml (½ tsp) bicarbonate
*   of soda*
2·5ml (½ tsp) cinnamon or
*   ground ginger (optional)*

1 large carrot
2 large eating apples
2 eggs
65ml (2½ fl oz) oil
*   of choice*

Place flour, bicarbonate of soda and spice of choice (if using) in a large bowl and mix well. Peel and dice carrot and one of the apples. Place in a blender or food processor together with the eggs. Run machine until mixture is smooth and fluffy. Add egg mixture to the flour together with the oil and gently fold in with a metal spoon. Finally, peel and dice the other apple and gently fold into sponge mixture. Spoon into 4 oiled ramekin dishes and bake at 190ºC, 375ºF, Gas Mark 5 for 20 minutes.

Gl Use brown rice flour or banana flour.
Gr Use banana flour.

⊞ Plain Sponge Pudding

115g (4 oz) milk-free margarine or 65ml (2½ fl oz) oil of choice	2 eggs, beaten
	175g (6 oz) brown rice flour, banana flour or barley flour
115g (4 oz) sugar or 65g (2½ oz) fructose	7·5ml (1½ tsp) gluten-free baking powder
	30ml (2 tbsp) water

For pudding made with margarine:
Cream margarine and sugar or fructose, and then add eggs. Mix together flour and baking powder and fold into mixture with water.
For pudding made with oil:
Sieve flour and baking powder together. Add all the rest of the ingredients and beat well.
To bake pudding:
Place mixture in a greased or oiled pudding basin and bake at 180°C, 350°F, Gas Mark 4 for 45–55 minutes. Serve with custard or 'Sweet Arrowroot Sauce' (see page 122).
To steam pudding:
Cover the filled basin with greaseproof paper and tie tightly with string and make a string handle. Steam in a large pan of boiling water for 1½–2 hours. Ensure that the pan does not boil dry. Serve as above.

 Gl Use brown rice flour or banana flour.
Gr Use banana flour.

⊞ Jam Sponge Pudding

Follow recipe and method for 'Plain Sponge Pudding'. Place 45ml (3 tbsp) jam or 'Fruit Filling' (see page 113) into the base of the dish and cover with the sponge mixture.

See Dietary Notes given for 'Plain Sponge Pudding'.

Eve's Pudding

Follow recipe and method for 'Plain Sponge Pudding' adding 2 peeled and diced apples to the sponge mixture.

See Dietary Notes given for 'Plain Sponge Pudding'.

Spotted Dick

Follow recipe and method for 'Plain Sponge Pudding' adding 50g (2 oz) natural currants or sultanas to the sponge mixture.

See Dietary Notes given for 'Plain Sponge Pudding'.

Chocolate Sponge Pudding

Follow recipe and method for 'Plain Sponge Pudding' using 160g (5½ oz) brown rice, banana or barley flour sieved together with 15g (½ oz) cocoa instead of the 175g (6 oz) flour. Serve with 'Chocolate Sauce' (see page 121).

See Dietary Notes given for 'Plain Sponge Pudding'.

Carob Sponge Pudding

Follow recipe and method for 'Plain Sponge Pudding' using 160g (5½ oz) brown rice, banana or barley flour sieved together with 15g (½ oz) carob powder instead of the 175g (6 oz) flour. Serve with 'Carob Sauce' (see page 121).

See Dietary Notes given for 'Plain Sponge Pudding'.

Date Sponge Pudding

Follow recipe and method for 'Plain Sponge Pudding' adding 50g (2 oz) chopped dates to the sponge mixture.

See Dietary Notes given for 'Plain Sponge Pudding'.

Fig Sponge Pudding

Follow recipe and method for 'Plain Sponge Pudding' adding 50g (2 oz) chopped dried figs to sponge mixture.

See Dietary Notes given for 'Plain Sponge Pudding'.

Fruit Filling (for puddings and crumbles)

225g (½ lb) fruit of choice
A little water
Sweetener of choice

15ml (1 tbsp) flour (use same flour as for pudding or crumble mixture)

Put fruit and a little water in saucepan and cook until soft. Mash with a fork. Sweeten to taste. Add flour mixed with a little water and stir while cooking until mixture thickens.

Gl Use gluten-free flour of choice.
Gr Use grain-free flour of choice.

Sago Fruit Crumble

½ quantity Fruit Filling (see previous recipe)
225g (8 oz) sago flour

100g (3½ oz) milk-free margarine
75g (3 oz) sugar

Brush the inside of a pie dish with melted margarine. Then place prepared fruit filling in the dish. Sieve the flour into a mixing bowl and rub in the margarine until the mixture resembles breadcrumbs. Stir in the sugar. Place the crumble mixture over the top of the fruit and smooth over with the back of a spoon. Bake at 180ºC, 350ºF, Gas Mark 4 for about 35 minutes or until the crumble is golden brown.

Tapioca Fruit Crumble

½ quantity Fruit Filling
  (see previous page)
225g (8 oz) tapioca flour

150g (5 oz) milk-free
  margarine
75g (3 oz) sugar

Follow method for 'Sago Fruit Crumble' substituting tapioca flour for sago flour to thicken fruit.

Almond and Apple Crumbles

3 medium-sized
  apples
15ml (1 tbsp) water
60ml (4 tbsp) unsulphured
  desiccated coconut
60ml (4 tbsp) ground almonds

75ml (5 tbsp) oil of choice
120ml (8 tbsp) millet flakes
  or buckwheat flakes
15–30ml (1–2 tbsp) sesame
  or sunflower seeds

Peel, core and slice apples and cook in 15ml (1 tbsp) water until soft. Place the apples in the bottom of 4 greased ramekin dishes. Combine all the rest of the ingredients thoroughly so that the oil is very well mixed. Sprinkle mixture over the fruit and bake at 180ºC, 350ºF, Gas Mark 4 for 20 minutes or until topping is golden.

Gl Use millet flakes or buckwheat flakes.
Gr Use buckwheat flakes.

Date Crumble

115g (4 oz) dates	50g (2 oz) milk-free
30ml (2 tbsp) water	margarine
115g (4 oz) brown rice flour	75g (3 oz) demerara sugar
or barley flour	or 50g (2 oz) fructose

Chop dates finely and put into a saucepan with the water. Simmer gently, stirring with a wooden spoon, until all liquid is absorbed and the mixture forms a smooth paste. Put into the bottom of a greased shallow dish and smooth with the back of a spoon. Rub together flour and margarine until it resembles breadcrumbs, and then stir in sugar or fructose. Put this mixture over the dates. Bake at 190°C, 375°F, Gas Mark 5 for 25–30 minutes.

Gl Use brown rice flour.

Apricot and Prune Pudding

Top this filling with one of the sponge or crumble mixtures to be found on the previous few pages.

115g (4 oz) unsulphured	50g (2 oz) walnuts
dried apricots	50g (2 oz) soft goats' cheese,
115g (4 oz) unsorbated	soft sheep's cheese or 'Curd
prunes	Cheese' (see page 185)
150ml (¼ pt) apple juice	25g (1 oz) sugar or 15g
or grape juice	(½ oz) fructose
1 lemon	

Put the apricots and prunes into a basin and pour the apple or grape juice over them. Add water until liquid just covers the fruit. Leave overnight. Finely grate the lemon rind and squeeze out the juice. Chop walnuts. In a small bowl, beat together the lemon rind, juice, cheese and sugar. Stir in the chopped walnuts. Drain the fruit, reserving the liquor, and remove the stones. Put half the fruit in the base of an ovenproof dish. Cover with the lemon cheese mixture and then cover with the remainder of the fruit. Top with a sponge or crumble mixture and bake at 180°C, 350°F, Gas Mark 4 for 45–55 minutes for a sponge or follow the baking instructions given for the type of crumble used. Use the drained liquor to make a sauce using 10ml (2 tsp) arrowroot to 300ml (½ pt) liquor.

E Use a crumble topping.
Gl Use gluten-free sponge or crumble topping.
Gr Use grain-free sponge or crumble topping.

⊞ Baked Barley Pudding

115g (4 oz) barley flakes
50g (2 oz) barley flour
50g (2 oz) demerara sugar
2·5ml (½ tsp) gluten-free
  baking powder
2·5ml (½ tsp) mixed spice
2·5ml (½ tsp) ground ginger
50g (2 oz) natural sultanas

50g (2 oz) ground almonds
25g (1 oz) vegetable suet
  with rice flour
2 eggs
30ml (2 tbsp) black treacle
150ml (¼ pt) goats' milk,
  sheep's milk, soya milk or
  'Nut Milk' (see page 188)

Mix all dry ingredients together. Stir in the vegetable suet. Beat eggs and add together with the milk and treacle. Mix well and place in a greased ovenproof dish. Bake at 190°C, 375°F, Gas Mark 5 for 1 hour; turn down heat to 180°C, 350°F, Gas Mark 4 and continue to cook for a further 45 minutes–1 hour until firm to the touch.

⊞ Apricot and Rye Pudding

50g (2 oz) unsulphured
  dried apricots
50g (2 oz) rye flakes
30ml (2 tbsp) clear honey

450ml (¾ pt) goats' milk
  or sheep's milk
1 egg, beaten

Place the apricots in a bowl, cover with water and leave overnight to soak. Purée the soaked apricots with 150ml (¼ pt) soaking liquor in a blender. Spoon into a shallow, greased or oiled ovenproof dish. Lightly toast the rye flakes. Mix together with 15ml (1 tbsp) honey, the milk and egg. Pour gently over the apricot purée. Stand the dish on a baking sheet and bake at 170°C, 325°F, Gas Mark 3 for about 45 minutes or until a skin has formed. Drizzle over the remainder of the honey and continue to bake for a further 15 minutes. Serve warm.

Prune and Barley Pudding

Follow recipe and method for 'Apricot and Rye Pudding' substituting prunes for apricots and barley flakes for rye flakes.

Creamed Rice Pudding

75g (3 oz) brown rice flakes
850ml (1½ pt) goats' milk
or sheep's milk
50g (2 oz) sugar or 40g
(1½ oz) fructose

Piece of vanilla pod or a
few drops of Bourbon
vanilla extract

(If using vanilla pod, leave in milk for a few minutes while it is hot and then remove.)
Bring the rice flakes and milk slowly to the boil in a saucepan. Cook gently for 8–10 minutes. Remove from heat and stir in rest of ingredients. This recipe makes a thin pudding. If you prefer a thicker pudding then use a little less milk.

Fruity Creamed Rice Pudding

Follow recipe for 'Creamed Rice Pudding' but use a little less milk to cook, then stir in chopped, canned or boiled fruit with some of the juice or chopped fresh fruit with its own juice.

Raisin 'n' Rice Pudding

Follow recipe for 'Creamed Rice Pudding' and add 50g (2 oz) natural raisins. Reduce the amount of sweetener by half.

Baked Rice Pudding

75g (3 oz) brown rice flakes
50g (2 oz) sugar or 25g
  (1 oz) fructose
850ml (1½ pt) goats' milk
  or sheep's milk

25g (1 oz) milk-free
  margarine
A little grated nutmeg
  (optional)

Put rice flakes, sugar or fructose and milk into a 1 litre (2 pt) pie dish. Leave for an hour, if possible, then stir well. Float knobs of margarine all over the top and place in oven at 150°C, 300°F, Gas Mark 2 for about ½ hour, or until pudding is rising in large bubbles all over. Lower heat to 140°C, 275°F, Gas Mark 1 and continue cooking for another ½ hour.

Grated nutmeg may be sprinkled over the pudding before baking, if desired.

 # Millet Pudding

450ml (¾ pt) hot goats' milk,
  sheep's milk or soya milk
45ml (3 tbsp) millet flakes
1 large egg, beaten
60ml (4 tbsp) honey or
  maple syrup

10ml (2 tsp) soya flour
2·5ml (½ tsp) ground
  nutmeg
Pinch of salt
450ml (¾ pt) cold milk (as
  above)

Mix the hot milk and millet flakes. In a separate container blend the rest of the ingredients, except the nutmeg, then combine the two mixtures and turn into greased or oiled custard cups or pie dish. Dust top with nutmeg. Bake at 180°C, 350°F, Gas Mark 4 until set, about 30 minutes.

Spicy Millet Pudding

575ml (1 pt) goats' milk,
  sheep's milk or soya milk
225g (8 oz) whole millet
5ml (1 tsp) ground cinnamon

50g (2 oz) muscovado or
  demerara sugar
30ml (2 tbsp) natural
  sultanas (optional)

Combine milk and millet with the spice and sugar in a saucepan. Bring to the boil and simmer for 10 minutes. Transfer to greased or oiled ovenproof dish, stir in dried fruit, if using, and bake at 180°C, 350°F, Gas Mark 4 for 20 minutes.

⊞ Fruit and Nut Millet Pudding

575ml (1 pt) goats' milk,
  sheep's milk or soya milk
100g (3½ oz) millet flakes
1 knob milk-free margarine
30ml (2 tbsp) sugar,
  honey or maple syrup

2 eggs, separated
Grated rind of 1 lemon
30ml (2 tbsp) natural
  raisins or sultanas
60ml (4 tbsp) ground
  almonds

Heat milk, millet flakes, and knob of margarine in a saucepan until boiling and then allow to cool. Add sugar, honey or maple syrup, egg yolks, lemon rind, raisins and nuts. Mix well. Finally, gently fold in stiffly-beaten egg whites. Put into a greased or oiled pie dish and bake at 200°C, 400°F, Gas Mark 6 for 20–25 minutes.

⊞ Baked Arrowroot Pudding

15ml (1 tbsp) arrowroot
15ml (1 tbsp) sugar or
  7·5ml (½ tbsp) fructose

575ml (1 pt) goats' milk,
  sheep's milk or soya milk
3 eggs

Put the arrowroot and sweetener of choice into a bowl. Add a little of the measured milk and mix well. Meanwhile, put the rest of the milk on to boil. Pour boiling milk over arrowroot, stirring all the time. Return to saucepan and heat, stirring all the time, until thick. Simmer gently for 2–3 minutes. Remove from heat, add beaten egg yolks and mix well. Whisk egg whites and fold into cooked mixture. Pour into an ovenproof dish and bake at 160°C, 325°F, Gas Mark 3 for ½ hour or until golden brown on top.

⬜E GlGr Apple Crisp

2 large cooking apples
50g (2 oz) natural sultanas
or natural raisins
75g (3 oz) milk-free
margarine

75g (3 oz) muscovado or
demerara sugar
150g (5 oz) porridge oats,
millet flakes or
buckwheat flakes

Peel and core apples, slice into a greased deep 22cm (8½") pie dish and add dried fruit. Cream together the margarine and sugar and then work in the flakes. Spread over the apples. Bake at 180°C, 350°F, Gas Mark 4 for 45 minutes or until crisp and golden brown. Serve hot or cold.

Gl Use millet flakes or buckwheat flakes.
Gr Use buckwheat flakes.

⬜E GlGr Baked Apples

4 large cooking apples
115g (4 oz) dates, finely
chopped, natural sultanas
or natural raisins
25g (1 oz) milk-free
margarine

45ml (3 tbsp) clear honey,
date syrup, maple syrup
or demerara sugar
A few blanched almonds,
shredded

Wash and core apples, score skin around middle with a knife. Place apples in an ovenproof dish and fill each one with dates, sultanas or raisins. Add a little water to the dish and spoon honey, syrup or sugar over each apple. Dot with a knob of milk-free margarine. Bake at 180°C, 350°F, Gas Mark 4 for 45 minutes, or until apples are tender. Baste apples with juice from the base of the dish and scatter shredded almonds on the top. Return to oven for a further 5 minutes to brown the almonds. Serve hot.

Rum and Raisin Sauce

175g (6 oz) natural raisins
45ml (3 tbsp) honey
Grated rind of 1 lemon
30ml (2 tbsp) lemon juice
225ml (8 fl oz) water

15ml (1 tbsp) cornflour
or arrowroot
30ml (2 tbsp) milk-free
margarine
30ml (2 tbsp) rum

Combine the raisins, honey, lemon rind and lemon juice. Mix the flour with the water and add to the mixture. Bring to the boil, stirring gently, and then simmer for 4–5 minutes. Stir in the margarine and rum. May be reheated for later use. Serve hot over puddings or pancakes.

Gr Use arrowroot.

 # Chocolate or Carob Sauce

25g (1 oz) cornflour or
arrowroot
15g (½ oz) cocoa powder
or carob powder
25g (1 oz) milk-free margarine

300ml (½ pt) goats' milk,
sheep's milk, soya milk
or 'Rice Dream'
25g (1 oz) sugar or 15g
(½ oz) fructose

Mix flour and cocoa or carob powder with a little of the milk. Bring the rest of the milk to the boil and pour over mixture, stirring well. Return to heat to thicken. Add margarine and stir well until melted, and then sweeten to taste. Serve hot with sponge pudding.

Gr Use arrowroot and goats', sheep's or soya milk.

 # Rich Chocolate Sauce

150g (5 oz) 'Green and
Black's Organic Dark
Chocolate'
5ml (1 tsp) milk-free
margarine

45ml (3 tbsp) date syrup,
or maple syrup
5ml (1 tsp) coffee granules
(optional)
150ml (¼ pt) 'Soya Creem'

Break chocolate into a small bowl and add margarine, syrup of choice and coffee granules (if using). Place bowl over a pan of boiling water and stir contents with a wooden spoon until chocolate has melted and sauce is smooth. Remove from heat and add 'Soya Creem' and beat well until mixture is again smooth.
To serve hot:
Return bowl to top of pan until sauce is hot. Serve immediately with chocolate sponge pudding.
To serve with ice cream:
Beat in a little water while sauce is hot to obtain the correct consistency.
To use as a very rich cake filling:
Leave in bowl undiluted until cold, by which time it will be thick.

⊞ Rich Carob Sauce

Follow recipe and method for 'Rich Chocolate Sauce' substituting 'Plamil Carob Confection' for the chocolate. Omit the syrup and coffee.

⊞ Sweet Arrowroot Sauce

15ml (1 tbsp) arrowroot
7·5ml (½ tbsp) sugar or
  5ml (1 tsp) fructose

300ml (½ pt) goats' milk,
  sheep's milk or soya milk

Put the arrowroot and sweetener of choice into a bowl or jug, add a little of the measured milk and mix well. Meanwhile, put the rest of the milk on to boil. Pour boiling milk over arrowroot, stirring all the time. Return mixture to saucepan and heat, stirring all the time, until thick. Simmer gently for 2–3 minutes.

⊞ Spiced Arrowroot Sauce

Follow recipe and method for 'Sweet Arrowroot Sauce' adding 15ml (1 tbsp) lemon juice and a pinch of nutmeg or cinnamon to taste.

Starters and Soups

Hummus

A tasty dip for parties. Serve with celery and carrot crudités and a choice of crispbreads which have been cut into fingers before baking.

225g (8 oz) chick peas
2 garlic cloves, crushed
30ml (2 tbsp) oil of choice
Juice of 1 large lemon
Salt and pepper to taste

60ml (4 tbsp) goats' yoghurt
  or sheep's yoghurt
Paprika to garnish
Chopped parsley to garnish

Soak the chick peas overnight in sufficient water to cover well. Drain. Place in a saucepan with just enough water to cover. Add the garlic cloves and bring to the boil, cover and simmer for 30 minutes. Allow to cool in the water. Put oil, lemon juice and yoghurt into blender or food processor. Add half the chick peas with the cooking liquor and garlic, and blend until smooth. Keep adding chick peas, along with some water if necessary, until they have all been incorporated. Season with salt and pepper to taste. Transfer to a serving dish, sprinkle with chopped parsley and paprika.

C If allowed lemon.

 Avocado Starter

225g (8 oz) mushrooms
30ml (2 tbsp) oil of choice
Soya Mayonnaise (see
   page 178)

2 avocado pears
4 small sprigs of parsley

Chop the mushrooms and sauté them in the oil. Drain well and allow to cool. Put them together with some soya mayonnaise into a bowl and mix well. You will need just enough mayonnaise to bind the mixture. Halve the avocado pears and remove the stones. Place each half on an individual dish. Pile mushroom mixture in the centres and garnish each with a sprig of parsley. Serve immediately.

Avocado Pâté

225g (8 oz) soft goats' cheese,
   soft sheep's cheese or 'Curd
   Cheese' (see page 185)
1 large ripe avocado pear

Juice of ½ lemon
Salt and pepper to taste
Flavouring: nutmeg or
   parsley

Sieve the cheese into a bowl. Peel the avocado and remove the stone. Chop the flesh and blend in a liquidiser or food processor with the lemon juice, salt, pepper, cheese and either a pinch of nutmeg or a little chopped parsley. Spoon into serving dish and chill until required. Serve each portion on a small plate with a few sprigs of watercress or a leaf or two of lettuce. Serve toast or crispbreads separately.

Watercress and Cheese Mousse

*60ml (2 tbsp) vegetable
  stock
15ml (1 tbsp) gelatine or
  7·5ml (1½ tsp) agar agar
2 bunches watercress
Salt and pepper to taste*

*115g (4 oz) homemade
  'Sheep's Curd Cheese' (see
  page 185)
60ml (4 tbsp) 'Mayonnaise'
  or 'Soya Mayonnaise' (see
  pages 177 & 178)
60ml (4 tbsp) sheep's yoghurt*

Dissolve gelatine or agar agar in the stock, according to the manufacturers' instructions, and then leave to cool. Wash the watercress well and trim off the coarse stems. Put into a food processor or blender together with the cooled stock and blend to a fine purée. Season to taste. Put the curd cheese and mayonnaise into a large bowl and beat until smooth and then fold in the yoghurt. Finally, add the purée to the cheese mixture and fold gently together until well mixed. Pour into a wetted ½ litre (1 pt) mould or into individual dishes and chill until set.

C Use homemade 'Curd Cheese' only if allowed lemon. Also use 'Soya Mayonnaise' and *'Kallo Yeast-free Vegetable Stock'*.
E Use 'Soya Mayonnaise'.

Stuffed Baby Beets

Serve as a first course or as a side salad.

*8 baby beetroots, cooked
115g (4 oz) soft goats' cheese
  or 'Curd Cheese' (see
  pages 185)
Chives*

*15–30ml (1–2 tbsp) goats'
  milk
Salt and pepper to taste
1 punnet Mustard and Cress*

Peel the skin from each beetroot. Scoop out the centre of each beetroot, taking care not to break the flesh. Chop the scooped out flesh. Place the cheese in a bowl, add chopped chives and blend in sufficient milk to obtain a smooth consistency. Add chopped beetroot and seasoning. Divide mixture between each baby beet, piling the mixture attractively on top. Top each with a sprinkling of chopped chives and serve on a bed of mustard and cress.

C Use homemade 'Curd Cheese' only if allowed lemon.

Grapefruit Mayonnaise

225g (8 oz) cucumber   *'Mustard and Yoghurt*
2 grapefruits   *Dressing' (see page 176)*
Frisée (endive)   *Chives, chopped*

Peel cucumber, cut into ½ lengthways, discard seeds and cut into dice. Peel grapefruits, divide into segments and remove all the membrane. Make little beds of frisée in 4 individual dishes and arrange cucumber and grapefruit on top. Drizzle Mustard and Yoghurt Dressing over and sprinkle with chopped chives. Chill until ready to serve.

Chilled Cucumber and Yoghurt Soup

A simple summer soup which requires no cooking.

350g (12 oz) goats' yoghurt   *2 spring onions, finely*
15cm (6") piece of cucumber,   *chopped*
*   grated*   *15ml (1 tbsp) fresh mint,*
15ml (1 tbsp) natural raisins,   *finely chopped*
*   finely chopped*   *60–90ml (4–6 tbsp) goats'*
8 walnut halves, finely   *milk*
*   chopped*   *Salt and pepper to taste*

Place yoghurt in a large bowl and stir in all the other ingredients. The amount of milk required will depend upon the thickness of the yoghurt. Chill for 1 hour. Stir. Put into individual soup bowls, and garnish each with a small sprig of mint.

Alternative:
If you wish to use sheep's yoghurt and milk instead of goats', then use less yoghurt and more milk to obtain the correct consistency.

Chilled Cucumber and Tofu Soup

Follow recipe and method for 'Chilled Cucumber and Yoghurt Soup' substituting silken tofu for yoghurt and soya milk for goats' milk. More soya milk may be needed to obtain the correct consistency.

Creamy Carrot Soup

This recipe shows how silken tofu may be used instead of cream.

450g (1 lb) carrots	300ml (½ pt) silken tofu
225g (8 oz) leeks, white part only	5ml (1 tsp) ground mace
	Salt and pepper to taste
600ml (1 pt) vegetable stock	

Scrub carrots and cut into slices and put into a saucepan together with shredded leeks. Cover with vegetable stock and simmer until completely tender. Allow to cool. Purée in a blender or food processor and, if smooth soup is required, rub through a fine sieve. Stir in the silken tofu and season to taste. Chill if it is to be served cold or, if serving hot, heat through gently but do not allow to boil.

C Use *'Kallo Yeast-free Vegetable Stock'*.

Creamy Turnip Soup

Follow recipe and method for 'Creamy Carrot Soup' substituting turnips for carrots.

Quick Scotch Broth

75g (3 oz) carrot
75g (3 oz) turnip
75g (3 oz) swede
Seasoning to taste

1 leek or small onion
30ml (2 tbsp) barley flakes
1·125 litres (2 pt) vegetable
   stock

Cut root vegetables into small dice, slice leek or chop onion. Add to saucepan together with flakes and stock. Bring to the boil, skim and simmer for 1 hour. Season to taste and serve.

C Use *'Kallo Yeast-free Vegetable Stock Cubes'*.

Polish Beetroot Soup

1 medium onion
1 large carrot
450g (1 lb) raw beetroot
7·5ml (½ tbsp) fresh parsley,
   chopped

1 bay leaf
Seasoning to taste
1·125 litres (2 pt) vegetable
   stock
1 egg white
Juice of ½ lemon

Peel and grate onion, carrot and beetroot. Put into large pan with parsley, bay leaf and stock. Simmer gently for 30 minutes. Pour through a sieve. Return to pan, whisk in egg white and simmer gently for a further 15 minutes. Strain again. Stir in lemon juice and season to taste. Serve hot.

·

Leek and Millet Soup

60ml (2 tbsp) olive oil
4 large leeks, sliced

115g (4 oz) whole millet
1·125 litres (2 pt) vegetable
   stock

Heat oil in a large, heavy-based pan and sweat the leeks for 10 minutes over low heat with the lid on. Add the millet and stock, bring to the boil and simmer for 20 minutes. Pour into a liquidiser or food processor and blend until smooth. Pour back into saucepan and reheat.

C Use *'Kallo Yeast-free Vegetable Stock Cubes'*.

⊞ Noodle Soup

1·5 litre (2½ pt) vegetable stock
50g (2 oz) carrot, diced
50g (2 oz) turnip, diced
30ml (2 tbsp) spring onions, finely chopped
50g (2 oz) spinach or pak choi, chopped
2·5cm (1") piece root ginger, finely chopped

50g (2 oz) courgette, deseeded and chopped
¼ cauliflower or some broccoli spears, broken into tiny florets
30ml (2 tbsp) tamari
25g (1 oz) Japanese rice noodles

Heat stock in a large saucepan and cook carrots and turnip for about 10 minutes. Add rest of ingredients, except the noodles, and continue to cook until vegetables are tender. Prepare the rice noodles as directed on the packet and stir into the soup just before serving. Season to taste.

⊞ Cream of Chestnut Soup

1 onion or leek
1 large carrot
2 sticks of celery
15ml (1 tbsp) oil of choice

325g (11 oz) kibbled chestnuts
1·125 litres (2 pt) vegetable stock
Salt and pepper to taste

Chop leek or peel and chop onion, carrot and celery. Heat oil in saucepan and sauté the chopped vegetables. Add kibbled chestnuts and stock and simmer gently for 1 hour. Purée in a blender or by rubbing through a sieve. Return to pan and add salt and pepper to taste. Reheat gently before serving.

C Use *'Kallo Yeast-free Vegetable Stock Cubes'*.

⬚ Rice and Tomato Soup

50g (2 oz) onion, chopped
2 sticks of celery, chopped
15g (½ oz) milk-free
  margarine
50g (2 oz) brown rice flakes
450g (1 lb) tomatoes,
  skinned and chopped
Salt and pepper to taste

½ bay leaf
2·5ml (½ tsp) ground mace
2·5ml (½ tsp) marjoram
  or basil, dried
575ml (1 pt) vegetable
  stock
150ml (¼ pt) goats' milk,
  sheep's milk or soya milk

Fry the onion and celery lightly in the margarine until soft and transparent. Add all the rest of the ingredients, except the milk, and simmer for 45 minutes. Remove the bay leaf. Rub through a sieve or process in a blender. Return to the pan together with the milk and reheat gently but do not allow to boil.

C Use 'Kallo Yeast-free Vegetable Stock Cube'.

⬚ Yellow Pea Soup

225g (8 oz) yellow split peas
15ml (1 tbsp) oil of choice
1 small onion, chopped
1 garlic clove, crushed
225g (8 oz) potatoes,
  scrubbed and cut up
1 small carrot, chopped

850ml (1½ pt) water
2 vegetable stock cubes
300ml (½ pt) goats' milk,
  sheep's milk or soya milk
Seasoning to taste
Chopped mint to garnish

Wash peas well, discarding dark ones which float. Soak overnight and then drain. Heat oil in a saucepan and sauté the onion and garlic until they are soft. Add drained peas, potatoes, carrot, water and stock cube. Simmer for about 1 hour, or until peas are tender. Rub through a sieve or purée in a food processor or blender. Return to pan, add milk, salt and pepper and reheat gently but do not allow to boil. Serve sprinkled with chopped mint.

C Use 'Kallo Yeast-free Vegetable Stock Cubes'.

Green Pea Soup

This makes a creamy textured soup. For a really thick soup, add a large scrubbed and chopped potato with the rest of the ingredients.

225g (8 oz) green split peas
15ml (1 tbsp) oil of choice
1 large onion or 2 leeks,
   chopped

1·125 litres (2 pt) water
2 vegetable stock cubes
2·5ml (½ tsp) celery salt
Salt and pepper to taste

Wash the peas well and then soak overnight. Drain. Heat oil in a saucepan and sauté the onion or leeks until soft. Add the drained peas, measured water and stock cubes. Stir until the stock cubes have dissolved, then simmer for 1 hour, or until green split peas are tender. Season with celery salt, salt and pepper to taste. Allow to cool a little and then purée in a blender or food processor until smooth. Reheat gently before serving.

C Use *'Kallo Yeast-free Vegetable Stock Cubes'.*

Haricot Bean Soup

225g (8 oz) haricot beans
1 large onion or 2 leeks
1 medium sized carrot
25g (1 oz) margarine or
   15ml (1 tbsp) olive oil
2 garlic cloves, crushed

850ml (1½ pt) water
30ml (2 tbsp) tomato purée
1 vegetable stock cube
Salt and pepper to taste
Chopped parsley to garnish

Wash beans and soak overnight. Drain. Chop onion or leek and dice carrots. Melt the fat and sauté the vegetables until onions are soft. Put the drained beans into a pan with all the rest of the ingredients, except the parsley. Simmer for 1 hour or until the beans are tender. Adjust seasoning to taste. Sprinkle with parsley.

C Use *'Kallo Yeast-free Vegetable Stock Cube'.*

Vegetables, Hot and Cold Savoury Dishes

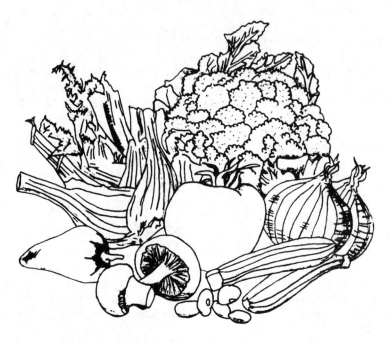

☐☐ Rye Dumplings

225g (8 oz) rye flour
5ml (1 tsp) bicarbonate
  of soda

Pinch of salt
40ml (8 tsp) olive oil
120ml (8 tbsp) cold water

Place dry ingredients in a bowl and add the oil and water. Mix to a dough. Divide into 12 equal portions and form into balls. Roll in a little rye flour. Float on top of casserole for the last 30 minutes of cooking time or float on top of a pan of gently simmering vegetables for 30 minutes.

Brown Rice Dumplings

Follow recipe and method for 'Rye Dumplings', substituting brown rice flour for rye flour.

Barley Dumplings

225g (8 oz) barley flour　　　　*Pinch of salt*
5ml (1 tsp) bicarbonate　　　　*40ml (8 tsp) oil of choice*
*　of soda*　　　　　　　　　　*150ml (10 tbsp) cold water*

Follow method for 'Rye Dumplings'.

Fennel with Chestnuts

225g (8 oz) fresh chestnuts　　　*1 large onion*
*　or 200g (7 oz) vacuum-*　　　　*2 large fennel bulbs*
*　packed whole chestnuts*　　　　*30ml (2 tbsp) olive oil*

To prepare fresh chestnuts:
Nick the skins with a pair of scissors and plunge into boiling water and blanch for 5 minutes. Remove one at a time and peel off both the shell and inner skin. Put prepared chestnuts into fresh water to just cover, bring to the boil and simmer for 40 minutes, then drain and set aside.

Peel and slice onion. Trim the fennel bulbs, wash well and then slice fairly thickly. Put together in a pan with oil and sauté for 5 minutes or so. Add the chestnuts and some of the cooking liquor or water and simmer for 10-15 minutes until fennel is tender.

C E Gl Gr **Cabbage Toss**

1 large onion
115g (4 oz) carrots
30ml (2 tbsp) olive oil
675g (1½ lb) cabbage

Salt and pepper to taste
40g (1½ oz) natural
    sultanas

Peel and chop onion. Peel carrots and cut into matchsticks. Shred the cabbage finely. Put oil into a large preheated frying pan or wok with a lid. Add the onion and carrot to pan and cook slowly without browning for 5 minutes. Add the cabbage to the pan. Toss the ingredients together in the pan, add seasoning, cover and cook gently for 15–20 minutes, turning occasionally. Remove from heat and add sultanas, mixing in well. Transfer to warmed serving dish.

C Omit sultanas.

C E Gl Gr **Marrow and Onions**

30ml (2 tbsp) vegetable oil
2 onions, sliced
1 large marrow, peeled
    and diced

575ml (1 pt) goats' milk
    or sheep's milk
Salt and pepper to taste
30ml (2 tbsp) cornflour or
    arrowroot

Heat oil in saucepan and sauté onion gently until transparent. Add diced marrow, milk and seasoning. Simmer gently until marrow is tender. Thicken with cornflour or arrowroot which has been blended with a little water. Season to taste. Goes well with 'Nut Burgers' (see page 151).

Gr Use arrowrooot.

Sweet Potato Marie

450g (1 lb) sweet potatoes
(white fleshed)

Milk-free margarine
Salt and pepper to taste

Wash sweet potatoes and boil in salted water until tender. Drain and peel when cooled. Mash with salt and pepper and a little milk-free margarine. Put into a small ovenproof dish and dot with milk-free margarine. Place under a hot grill until golden or bake at 180°C, 350°F, Gas Mark 4 until golden.

 # Sweet Potato Cakes

2 medium-sized sweet potatoes
(white fleshed)
15ml (1 tbsp) oil of choice

30g (1 oz) walnuts or
pecans, finely chopped
Salt and pepper to taste

Peel and dice sweet potato and cook in salted water for 8–12 minutes or until just tender. Drain and leave until cold. Mash and then stir in chopped nuts. Divide into 4 portions and form into round cakes about 1·25cm (½") thick. Heat oil in frying pan and cook the cakes for approximately 5 minutes on each side until browned. (Can be rolled in flour or flakes before frying to give a crunchy coating.)

Gl Use gluten-free flour or flakes of choice.
Gr Use grain-free flour or flakes of choice.

 # Vegetable Cakes

3 courgettes
Salt
1 large sweet potato
(white fleshed)
2 carrots

1 spring onion
5ml (1 tsp) fresh thyme,
finely chopped
Any flour of choice
15ml (1 tbsp) vegetable oil

Grate courgettes, sprinkle with salt and set aside for 30 minutes.

Meanwhile, peel and chop sweet potato and cook in salted water for 8–12 minutes or until just tender. Drain well and mash. Drain the courgettes and pat dry. Grate the carrot and slice the spring onion. Mix all vegetables together, add thyme and season to taste. Shape into eight cakes and coat in flour of choice. Fry until golden brown on each side.

Gl Use gluten-free flour of choice.
Gr Use grain-free flour of choice.

Roast Sweet Potatoes

450g (1 lb) sweet potatoes   *30ml (2 tbsp) olive oil*
*   (orange fleshed)*   *Salt and pepper to taste*

Wash sweet potatoes and trim off any hairs. Pat dry. Cut each one into 4 slices lengthways and then cut each slice in half. Place in a bowl and coat well with oil. Season to taste. Place singly on a baking sheet and roast at 220ºC, 425ºF, Gas Mark 7 for 40 minutes.

Pease Pudding

450g (1 lb) split peas   *Yolk of 1 standard egg*
2·5ml (½ tsp) salt   *Salt and pepper to taste*
15g (½ oz) milk-free
*   margarine*

Soak the peas overnight. Drain. Put into a saucepan and cover with fresh water. Add salt and bring slowly to the boil. Cover and simmer gently for 2 hours, stirring occasionally. Add a little extra boiling water if peas begin to get too dry. Rub through a sieve or purée in a blender. Add margarine and egg yolk. Mix well. Season to taste. Transfer to a 500ml (1 pt) greased ovenproof dish and bake at 180ºC, 350ºF, Gas Mark 4 for 30 minutes.

Courgettes Provençale

900g (2 lb) courgettes
1 onion
60ml (4 tbsp) olive oil
350g (12 oz) tomatoes
Salt and pepper to taste

15ml (1 tbsp) fresh basil, chopped
75g (3 oz) hard goats' or hard sheep's cheese, grated or 'Parmazano'

Cut courgettes into 0·75cm (¼") slices, discarding the ends. Peel and chop onion. Heat oil in a saucepan and add courgettes and onion. Cook for 8–10 minutes or until just tender, stirring occasionally. Drain and arrange courgettes in overlapping circles in a large shallow ovenproof dish. Slice tomatoes and fry briefly, but do not allow to go soft. Add salt, pepper and basil. Arrange in one overlapping circle over courgettes. Sprinkle with grated cheese or 'Parmazano' and bake at 190°C, 375°F, Gas Mark 5 for 25 minutes until golden brown.

Leek and Sweet Potato Gratin

450g (1 lb) leeks
450g (1 lb) sweet potatoes (white fleshed)
150g (5 oz) Roquefort cheese
225g (8 oz) sheep's yoghurt

25g (1 oz) plain breadcrumbs or soda breadcrumbs, any type (see pages 26-42)
Salt and pepper to taste

Trim and slice leeks. Peel sweet potatoes and slice thinly. Rinse, drain and dry on kitchen paper. Arrange sliced sweet potato and leeks in a large shallow ovenproof dish and season lightly. Crumble roquefort into a bowl and blend in yoghurt to a smooth sauce. Pour the sauce over the vegetables and sprinkle with breadcrumbs. Bake at 180°C, 350°F, Gas Mark 4 for 35–40 minutes or until golden brown. Serve immediately.

C̲ Use soda breadcrumbs of choice.
G̲l̲ Use gluten-free breadcrumbs of choice.
G̲r̲ Use grain-free breadcrumbs of choice.

C E Gl □ **Nutty Pilaff**

1 onion, chopped
1 clove garlic, crushed
30ml (2 tbsp) olive oil
225g (8 oz) long-grain brown
  rice or whole millet
750ml (1¼ pt) vegetable
  stock
Pinch of turmeric powder
50g (2 oz) natural raisins
  or natural sultanas

1 bay leaf
Salt and pepper to taste
50g (2 oz) cooked peas
50g (2 oz) cashews or
  pine kernels
115g (4 oz) mushrooms
  or 4 hard-boiled eggs
Paprika to garnish eggs
Fresh parsley or mint,
  chopped

Peel, slice and finely chop onion. Fry the garlic and onion in olive oil until tender, but not brown. Wash rice or millet and stir into pan and cook for 1 minute. Stir in turmeric and gradually add stock. Then add sultanas or raisins, bay leaf and seasoning. Cover pan and simmer for 30–35 minutes for the rice or 20 minutes for the whole millet, stirring occasionally until tender. Stir in the peas and nuts and adjust seasoning if necessary. Meanwhile, fry or grill the mushrooms or shell hard-boiled eggs and cut in half lengthwise. Pile pilaff onto a warmed serving dish. Place mushrooms or egg halves around the edge and sprinkle each egg with paprika. Garnish with chopped parsley or mint.

C   Use *'Kallo Yeast-free Vegetable Stock Cube'* and omit dried
    fruit and mushrooms.
E   Use mushrooms.

C E Gl Gr **Salsify (or Scorzonera) au Gratin**

450g (1 lb) young salsify or
  scorzonera roots
Salt
15ml (1 tbsp) arrowroot or
  cornflour
300ml (½ pt) goats' milk
  or sheep's milk

115g (4 oz) hard goats'
  cheese or hard sheep's
  cheese, grated
Pinch of nutmeg, paprika,
  cayenne or chilli powder
3 large tomatoes or
  mushrooms, sliced

Scrub the salsify or scorzonera thoroughly. Cook in boiling salted water for 40–45 minutes until tender. Drain thoroughly, peel the skins off and put the roots into an oiled ovenproof dish. Mix the arrowroot or cornflour with a little of the measured milk. Bring the rest of the milk to the boil. Pour over mixed flour, stirring well, and return to the pan. Bring back to the boil and cook for 2–3 minutes. Add two thirds of the cheese and season to taste. Pour over vegetables. Arrange slices of tomato or mushroom on top and sprinkle with remaining cheese. Either brown under the grill or bake at 190°C, 375°F, Gas Mark 5 for 15 minutes.

C Use tomatoes.
Gr Use arrowroot.

 ## Stuffed Peppers

45–60ml (3–4 tbsp) oil of choice
1 onion, chopped
75g (3 oz) button mushrooms
175g (6 oz) long-grain brown
   rice, Camargue red rice, whole
   millet or buckwheat groats
4 tomatoes

400ml (14 fl oz) vegetable
   stock
15ml (1 tbsp) fresh parsley,
   chopped
Salt and pepper to taste
4 large even-sized peppers
4 sprigs of parsley to garnish

Heat oil in pan and fry onion until soft. Add mushrooms and rice, millet or buckwheat and cook gently for 1–2 minutes. Add stock and simmer, covered, for approximately 30 minutes for the rice or buckwheat or 15–20 minutes for the millet. Drain off any excess liquid. Add chopped skinned tomatoes and parsley. Season to taste. Meanwhile, cut a slice off the top of each pepper at stalk end. Scoop out seeds and pith. Place in a large pan of boiling water and leave for 2–3 minutes to blanch. Lift out and drain. Brush outsides with a little oil and set on an ovenproof dish. Divide filling into four and fill each pepper. Cover with kitchen foil or a lid and bake at 190°C, 375°F, Gas Mark 5 for 20 minutes.

Gr Use buckwheat groats.

Fried Stuffed Cucumber

2 large cucumbers
60ml (4 tbsp) cornflour or
  arrowroot
425g (15 oz) butter beans,
  cooked
1 egg or 10ml (2 tsp) 'Cirrus
  HPMC Egg Replacer'
  and 90ml (6 tbsp) water
10ml (2 tsp) tamari
Pinch of salt
10ml (2 tsp) spring onions,
  finely chopped

20ml (4 tsp) fresh root
  ginger, finely chopped
Plain breadcrumbs or
  soda breadcrumbs, any
  type (see pages 26-42)
30ml (2 tbsp) olive oil

For the sauce:
300ml (½ pt) vegetable stock
15ml (1 tbsp) tamari
30ml (2 tbsp) fresh parsley,
  finely chopped

Cut unpeeled cucumber into 2·5cm (1") thick slices and remove centres with an apple corer. Lightly dust hollow interiors with cornflour or arrowroot (reserve remainder). Drain butter beans well and place in food processor together with egg (if using), 10 ml (2 tsp) tamari and pinch of salt. Blend until beans are well broken up. Tip into a mixing bowl and add chopped spring onions and ginger. This stuffing will be too slack, so add sufficient breadcrumbs to obtain the correct consistency. Fill the centres of cucumber pieces with the stuffing and dip ends into cornflour or arrowroot to seal in the stuffing. Form any remaining stuffing into nugget-sized balls and coat these in cornflour or arrowroot. Heat oil in frying pan and fry balls and stuffed cucumber slices until nicely browned. Add vegetable stock and 15ml (1 tbsp) tamari to pan, bring to the boil, cover and simmer until cucumber is tender and filling cooked through. Thicken sauce with remaining cornflour or arrowroot which has been mixed with a little water. Serve sprinkled with chopped parsley and accompanied by boiled rice, whole millet or buckwheat groats (see page 147 for cooking instructions).

To make with egg replacer:
Mix the egg replacer with some of the breadcrumbs and then add the water. Add this mixture to the stuffing together with the spring onions and ginger.

E Use *'Cirrus HPMC Egg Replacer'*.
Gl Use gluten-free breadcrumbs of choice.
Gr Use arrowroot and grain-free breadcrumbs of choice. Serve with buckwheat groats

Glazed Onions with Maize Stuffing

3 cups 'Maizemeal Bread',
  crumbed (see page 37)
4 Spanish onions (about
  350g (12 oz) each)
120ml (8 tbsp) milk-free
  margarine
Salt and black pepper to taste

240ml (8 fl oz) maple
  syrup
300ml (½ pt) vegetable
  stock
4 sticks celery with leaves
115g (4 oz) natural raisins
  or natural sultanas

Spread maizemeal breadcrumbs on a baking tray and put in a warm oven to dry out while you prepare the other ingredients. Lightly grease an ovenproof dish. Peel onions and cut in half crosswise. Scoop out onion centres with a spoon, being careful to leave the shells with 1cm (¼") at the sides and 1·5cm (½") at the base. Reserve remaining centres for the stuffing. Place the onion shells in prepared ovenproof dish. Smear the shells, inside and out, with half of the margarine. Spoon 30ml (2 tbsp) syrup into each shell and pour half the vegetable stock into the bottom of the dish and cover with a lid. Bake at 180°C, 350°F, Gas Mark 4 for 15 minutes. Uncover and baste upper edges with syrup from inside the cavities of the onions. Continue baking uncovered until tender, about a further 15 minutes.

To make the stuffing:

Heat the remaining margarine in the frying pan and sauté the chopped onion for 1 minute. Chop celery finely and add to onion and continue to sauté until vegetables are soft. Stir in the sultanas or raisins. Remove from heat and add maizemeal breadcrumbs and then stir in sufficient vegetable stock to hold stuffing together when scooped with a spoon. Season to taste. Mould stuffing into balls and stuff into onion cavities. Baste with liquid from base of dish and bake for a further 15 minutes.

Glazed Onions with Millet Stuffing

Follow recipe and method for 'Glazed Onions with Maize Stuffing' using 'Millet Batter Bread' (see page 37) instead of 'Maizemeal Bread'.

Glazed Onions with Rice Stuffing

Follow recipe and method for Glazed Onions with Maize Stuffing using 'Brown Rice Batter Bread' (see page 37) instead of 'Maizemeal Bread'.

Stuffed Aubergines

4 medium-sized aubergines
4 large tomatoes
1 medium-sized onion
25g (1 oz) milk-free
margarine
Salt and black pepper to taste

115g (4 oz) hard goats'
cheese or hard sheep's
cheese, grated
50g (2 oz) plain breadcrumbs
or soda breadcrumbs, any
type (see pages 26-42)

Remove stalks from aubergines, place in a large saucepan and cover with water. Bring to the boil, cover, and simmer for 15 minutes. Drain. Cut aubergines in half lengthwise. Scoop out flesh and chop. Place aubergine shells in a shallow ovenproof dish. Put tomatoes in a bowl and cover with boiling water. Leave for 1 minute, drain, skin and chop. Peel and chop onion finely. Melt margarine in frying pan and add chopped onion and aubergine. Fry for 5 minutes and then stir in chopped tomatoes and continue to fry gently for a minute or so. Remove from heat. Cut cheese into 1·25cm (½") cubes and add to mixture with the rest of the ingredients. Fill aubergine shells and cook in centre of oven at 180°C, 350°F, Gas Mark 4 for 30–40 minutes or until tender and golden.

C Use soda breadcrumbs of choice.
Gl Use gluten-free breadcrumbs of choice.
Gr Use grain-free breadcrumbs of choice.

C Gl Gr Leek and Hazelnut Loaf

30ml (2 tbsp) olive oil
1 large leek, chopped
1 large carrot, grated
115g (4 oz) plain breadcrumbs
  or soda breadcrumbs, any
  type (see pages 26-42)
115g (4 oz) hazelnuts, ground
  or very finely chopped

Salt and pepper to taste
5ml (1 tsp) fresh thyme,
  chopped
15ml (1 tbsp) fresh parsley,
  chopped
2 eggs, beaten
Up to 200ml (7 fl oz)
  vegetable stock

Sauté leeks and carrots in the olive oil for a few minutes until they begin to soften. Stir in breadcrumbs, hazelnuts, seasoning, herbs and beaten eggs. Add stock a little at a time until mixture holds together well. Spoon into an oiled Pyrex loaf dish. Bake at 180°C, 350°F, Gas Mark 4 for 40 minutes. Turn out and serve hot or cold. (Makes a good pâté to serve with biscuits or on bread. Can also be cooked in ramekins.)

C Use 'Kallo Yeast-free Vegetable Stock Cube' and soda breadcrumbs.
Gl Use gluten-free breadcrumbs of choice.
Gr Use grain-free breadcrumbs of choice.

C Gl Gr Leek and Cheese Loaf

Follow recipe and method for 'Leek and Hazelnut Loaf' substituting 115g (4 oz) hard goats' cheese or hard sheep's cheese for hazelnuts.

See Dietary Notes for 'Leek and Hazelnut Loaf'.

Millet Croquettes

225g (8 oz) millet flakes
575ml (1 pt) water
15ml (1 tbsp) olive oil
1 onion, finely chopped
15ml (1 tbsp) parsley,
   chopped

2 eggs, beaten
Salt and pepper to taste
30–45ml (2–3 tbsp)
   hard goats' cheese or
   hard sheep's cheese,
   grated or 'Parmazano'

Combine millet flakes with water and simmer gently, stirring continuously until thick. Remove from the heat and leave in pan until cool. Fry the onion in the oil. Mix the fried onion, parsley, beaten eggs, seasoning and grated cheese or *'Parmazano'* with the millet. Shape into rolls and fry until golden brown.

C Use goats' cheese or sheep's cheese.

 # Carrot and Cheese Savoury

4 large carrots, grated
2 large onions, grated
225g (8 oz) buckwheat flakes,
   millet flakes or porridge oats
175g (6 oz) hard goats' cheese
   or hard sheep's cheese, grated

5ml (1 tsp) dried oregano
Salt and pepper to taste
300ml (½ pt) goats' milk
   or sheep's milk
115g (4 oz) milk-free
   margarine

Mix together grated carrot and onion. In a separate bowl mix together flakes, cheese, oregano and seasoning. Grease or oil a deep ovenproof dish. Arrange alternate layers of the two mixtures in the dish, starting and finishing with the cheese mixture. Pour milk over and dot with margarine. Place high up in oven and bake at 200°C, 400°F, Gas Mark 6 for about 30 minutes or until golden brown. Serve hot or cold with green salad.

Gl Use buckwheat flakes or millet flakes.
Gr Use buckwheat flakes.

Pepper and Millet Timbales

4 red peppers
30ml (2 tbsp) olive oil
1 onion, finely chopped
1 garlic clove, finely
   chopped

225g (8 oz) whole millet
575ml (1 pt) vegetable stock
30ml (2 tbsp) fresh
   coriander or parsley,
   chopped

Place peppers on a baking sheet and brush with a little olive oil. Bake for 20 minutes at 200°C, 400°F, Gas Mark 6. Peel the roasted peppers, deseed and cut two circles from each pepper with a 7·5cm (3") pastry cutter. Dice the trimmings. Sauté the onion and garlic in the rest of the oil until just softened. Stir in the diced pepper, whole millet and vegetable stock and cook for 15–20 minutes until millet is tender and stock has been absorbed. Add coriander or parsley and season to taste. Grease 4 ramekin dishes and place one red pepper disc in the base of each one. Divide the millet mixture between the four dishes, press down well and smooth tops. Finally place another red pepper disc on top of each dish. (Can be prepared to this stage in advance.)* Bake at 200°C, 400°F, Gas Mark 6 for 15 minutes. Run a knife round each ramekin to loosen. Invert onto serving plates and unmould. Serve as part of a main course.

This quantity will serve six people as a starter cooked in dariole moulds and served with a salad of mixed leaves.

[C] Use 'Kallo Yeast-free Vegetable Stock Cube'.

Leek and Millet Timbales

2 large leeks
30ml (2 tbsp) olive oil
225g (8 oz) whole millet

575ml (1 pt) vegetable stock
30ml (2 tbsp) fresh coriander
   or parsley, chopped

Slit leeks lengthways and then slice. Place in a pan with oil and sauté over low heat until softened. Add millet and stock and cook for 15–20 minutes until millet is tender and stock is absorbed. Add herbs and divide between four greased ramekins. Continue as for 'Pepper and Millet Timbales' from the *.

[C] Use 'Kallo Yeast-free Vegetable Stock Cube'.

Stir-fried Rice Noodles with Pak Choi and Broccoli

115g (4 oz) stir-fry rice noodles
250g (9 oz) broccoli florets
15ml (1 tbsp) olive oil
2·5cm (1") root ginger,
  finely chopped
4 spring onions, chopped

200g (7 oz) pak choi,
  chopped
115ml (4 fl oz) vegetable
  stock
15ml (1 tbsp) tamari
Sesame seeds to taste
  (optional)

Place the rice noodles in a large bowl and pour boiling water over them to cover. Steep for 4 minutes, drain and rinse with cold water and then drain well. Lay out to dry for 15 minutes. Blanch broccoli florets in boiling water for a few minutes only. Drain and rinse in cold water and then drain well. Heat oil in preheated wok or large heavy frying pan, add ginger and spring onions and stir-fry for 2–3 minutes. Add pak choi and stir-fry for 3 minutes. Then add the noodles, stock, tamari and broccoli spears and cook for 2 minutes, or until the noodles and broccoli are thoroughly reheated. Sprinkle with sesame seeds, if desired. Serve at once.

 ## Spicy Vegetables with Whole Millet or Buckwheat Groats

1 red pepper
45ml (3 tbsp) olive oil
1 onion, chopped
1 clove garlic, crushed
30ml (1 tbsp) garam masala
400g (14 oz) cannellini beans
  or chick peas, cooked
1 fennel bulb, sliced
2 courgettes, sliced

15ml (1 tbsp) sun-dried
  tomato paste
300ml (½ pt) vegetable
  stock
Salt and pepper to taste
225g (8 oz) whole millet
  or buckwheat groats
Fresh coriander, chopped

Cut pepper into pieces and discard seeds. Char the pepper, skin side up, under the grill. Leave until cool enough to handle and then take off the skin and cut into strips. Heat the oil in a large pan and sauté the onion and garlic until soft. Stir in the garam masala and cook for 1 minute. Add the well-drained cannellini beans or chick peas with the prepared fennel and courgettes. Stir the sun-dried tomato paste into the stock and add to pan along with salt and pepper. Bring to the boil and simmer for 12 minutes. Add the prepared red pepper and cook for a further few minutes until vegetables are tender. Serve with millet or buckwheat and garnished with fresh coriander.

To cook the millet:
Place the millet in a pan with water, bring to the boil and simmer, covered for 15–20 minutes until millet is tender. Drain.

To cook the buckwheat:
Heat 5ml (1 tsp) oil in a pan and fry buckwheat over medium heat for about 3 minutes or until it just begins to brown. Pour over boiling water, bring back to the boil and simmer, covered, for 20 minutes or until buckwheat is tender. Drain.

C Use *'Kallo Yeast-free Vegetable Stock Cube'*.
Gr Use buckwheat groats.

CE Gl Savoury Crumble

This tasty topping turns a dish of cooked vegetables into a meal. Any vegetables can be used, with or without a sauce.

50g (2 oz) brown rice
   flour
50g (2 oz) milk-free
   margarine
Salt and pepper to taste

50g (2 oz) nuts, any type
50g (2 oz) buckwheat flakes,
   millet flakes or porridge oats
Handful sunflower seeds

Place the vegetables in the bottom of an ovenproof dish and coat with sauce, if using. Place the flour into a mixing bowl and rub in the fat with the fingertips, until it resembles breadcrumbs. Add seasoning. Grind the nuts in a blender or food processor. Stir into mixture along with the flakes. Spread mixture over the vegetables and scatter sunflower seeds over the top. Bake at 180°C, 350°F, Gas Mark 4 for 20 minutes.

Gl Use millet flakes or buckwheat flakes.
Gr Use buckwheat flakes.

C E Gl Gr Lentil Savoury Mix

This mixture can be used for 'Lentil Roast', 'Lentil Croquettes', or 'Lentil Burgers', or to fill pies or pasties.

225g (8 oz) green lentils
50g (2 oz) milk-free
  margarine or 30ml
  (2 tbsp) vegetable oil
1 onion or leek, chopped
2 large tomatoes, skinned
  or 2 courgettes, sliced
1 small apple, peeled,
  cored and chopped
  or 1 carrot, grated

50g (2 oz) plain breadcrumbs
  or soda breadcrumbs, any
  type (see pages 26–42)
5ml (1 tsp) fresh thyme,
  chopped
10ml (2 tsp) fresh parsley,
  chopped
Salt and pepper to taste

Soak the lentils overnight in cold water. Drain. Put them into saucepan and cover with fresh water. Bring to the boil and simmer gently until they are soft and all the water has been absorbed. Mash them well with a potato masher. Heat the fat and fry the onion or leek, vegetables and fruit until quite soft. Add the lentils, together with the breadcrumbs, herbs and season to taste.

C Use soda breadcrumbs of choice and carrot.
Gl Use gluten-free breadcrumbs of choice.
Gr Use grain-free breadcrumbs of choice.

C E Gl Gr Lentil Roast

Use 'Lentil Savoury Mix'. Press the mixture into a greased Pyrex loaf dish. Cover with greaseproof paper or foil and bake at 190°C, 375°F, Gas Mark 5 for 1 hour.

Lentil Croquettes

Use 'Lentil Savoury Mix'. Divide the mixture into portions and roll into shape with your hands. Coat in breadcrumbs (same type as used for savoury mix) and fry in oil until golden brown all over.

Lentil Burgers

Use 'Lentil Savoury Mix'. Divide the mixture into portions and shape into rounds. Flatten tops and fry in oil until golden on both sides.

Haricot Bean Savoury Mix

Follow recipe and method for 'Lentil Savoury Mix' substituting haricot beans for green lentils. Use to fill pies or pasties or as described below.

See Dietary Notes given for 'Lentil Savoury Mix'.

Haricot Bean Roast

Use 'Haricot Bean Savoury Mix'. Press the mixture into a greased Pyrex loaf dish. Cover with greaseproof paper or foil and bake at 190°C, 375°F, Gas Mark 5 for 1 hour.

Haricot Bean Croquettes

Use 'Haricot Bean Savoury Mix'. Divide the mixture into portions and roll into shape with your hands. Coat in breadcrumbs (same type as used for savoury mix) and fry in oil until golden brown all over.

Haricot Bean Burgers

Use 'Haricot Bean Savoury Mix'. Divide the mixture into portions and shape into rounds. Flatten tops and fry until golden brown on both sides.

Yellow Pea Savoury Mix

Follow recipe and method for 'Lentil Savoury Mix' substituting yellow split peas for green lentils. Use to fill pies or pasties or as described below.

See Dietary Notes given for 'Lentil Savoury Mix'.

Yellow Pea Roast

Use 'Yellow Pea Savoury Mix'. Press the mixture into a greased Pyrex loaf dish. Cover with greaseproof paper or foil and bake at 190°C, 375°F, Gas Mark 5 for 1 hour.

Yellow Pea Croquettes

Use 'Yellow Pea Savoury Mix'. Divide the mixture into portions and roll into shape with your hands. Coat in breadcrumbs (same type as used for savoury mix) and fry in oil until golden brown all over.

C|E G|G| **Yellow Pea Burgers**

Use 'Yellow Pea Savoury Mix'. Divide the mixture into portions and shape into rounds. Flatten tops and fry in oil until golden brown on both sides.

C|E G|G| **Nut Burgers**

225g (8 oz) walnuts, pecans
  or hazelnuts, ground
2 medium-sized carrots,
  grated
115g (4 oz) plain breadcrumbs
  or soda breadcrumbs, any
  type (see pages 26–42)
15ml (1 tbsp) fresh parsley,
  chopped

5ml (1 tsp) fresh thyme,
  chopped
Salt and black pepper to taste
1 vegetable stock cube
90ml (6 tbsp) boiling water
40ml (8 tsp) olive oil
1 large egg, beaten or 10ml
  (2 tsp) 'Cirrus HPMC Egg
  Replacer' and 90ml
  (6 tbsp) water

Place the carrot, ground nuts and breadcrumbs into a large mixing bowl. Stir in herbs, salt and pepper. Dissolve stock cube in the boiling water and add this to the nut mixture together with the oil and the beaten egg. Mix well. Divide into 4 equal portions, mould into desired shapes and place in hot frying pan coated with a little olive oil. Fry until browned and then turn and brown other side. Serve hot with leek or apple sauce.

To make with egg replacer:
Mix egg replacer with some of the breadcrumbs and then add the water. Add to the nut mixture together with the oil.

C Use *'Kallo Yeast-free Vegetable Stock Cube'* and soda
    breadcrumbs of choice.
E Use *'Cirrus HPMC Egg Replacer'*.
G| Use gluten-free breadcrumbs of choice.
Gr Use grain-free breadcrumbs of choice.

Cheese and Bean Burgers

275g (10 oz) butter beans,
  cooked or tinned
3 eggs
175g (6 oz) plain breadcrumbs
  or soda breadcrumbs, any
  type (see pages 26–42)
22ml (1½ tbsp) olive oil
Salt and black pepper to taste

30ml (2 tbsp) fresh parsley,
  chopped
5ml (1 tsp) fresh thyme,
  chopped
150g (5 oz) hard goats'
  cheese or hard sheep's
  cheese, grated

Drain butter beans well, place in a food processor together with eggs and 22ml (1½ tbsp) olive oil and blend. Pour into a large mixing bowl and add the rest of the ingredients. Mix well and leave to stand for a few minutes. Heat oil in a large frying pan. Divide mixture into 8 equal portions, mould into shape with hands and fry until golden brown on both sides.

C Use soda breadcrumbs of choice.
Gl Use gluten-free breadcrumbs of choice.
Gr Use grain-free breadcrumbs of choice.

 # Tofu Burgers

175g (6 oz) leeks
115g (4 oz) carrots
115g (4 oz) mushrooms
5ml (1 tsp) olive oil
5ml (1 tsp) oregano
50g (2 oz) millet flakes
  or buckwheat flakes

225g (8 oz) tofu, thoroughly
  drained and mashed
30ml (2 tbsp) tahini
30ml (2 tbsp) tamari
Salt and pepper to taste
40g (1½ oz) sesame seeds

Chop the leeks, coarsely grate the carrot and slice the mushrooms. Put the oil into a heavy-based pan and heat. Add the prepared vegetables and sauté for about 8 minutes. Remove from the heat, add oregano, flakes, tofu, tahini, tamari and season with salt and pepper. Stir the mixture well and then leave to cool for a few minutes. Divide the mixture into 8 portions and mould each one into a ball. Roll each ball in sesame seeds until well covered, and then flatten each ball into a burger shape with a potato masher or the palm of the hand. Grill or fry for about 5 minutes on each side.

Gr Use buckwheat flakes.

C E Gl Gluten-free Macaroni Cheese

225g (8 oz) gluten-free
macaroni, corn pasta or
rice and millet pasta
5ml (1 tsp) 'Grey
Poupon Mustard' or
'Mustard' (see page 183)
Salt and pepper to taste

60ml (4 tbsp) cornflour
or arrowroot
575ml (1 pt) goats' milk
or sheep's milk
225g (8 oz) hard goats'
cheese or hard sheep's
cheese, grated

Cook the pasta as directed on packet, taking care not to overcook it. Drain. Mix the mustard and cornflour or arrowroot with 60ml (4 tbsp) of the measured milk. Pour the rest of the milk into a saucepan and bring to the boil. Pour over the cornflour or arrowroot mixture and stir very well. Return to pan and bring back to the boil, stirring all the time, until sauce is thick and smooth. Simmer for 1 minutes. Season to taste. Stir in the pasta and about three quarters of the cheese. Pour into an ovenproof dish and sprinkle with the rest of the cheese. Place under a hot grill until the top is golden brown.

C Use vinegar-free mustard or leave mustard out altogether.

C Gl Gluten-free Spaghetti Soufflé

175g (6 oz) gluten-free
spaghetti, corn spaghetti
or rice spaghetti
50g (2 oz) cornflour or
arrowroot
575ml (1 pt) goats' milk
or sheep's milk

225g (8 oz) hard goats'
cheese or hard sheep's
cheese, grated
4 eggs, separated
Chives or spring onion,
chopped
Salt and pepper to taste

Cook the spaghetti as directed on the pack, taking care not to overcook it, and drain. Mix the cornflour or arrowroot with a little of the milk and bring the rest of the milk to nearly boiling point. Pour over the cornflour or arrowroot mixture, stirring well and return to pan. Heat gently and simmer for 2–3 minutes. Remove from the heat and stir in grated cheese, egg yolks, chives or spring onion and cooked spaghetti. Season to taste and finally fold in stiffly-beaten egg whites. Bake in a soufflé dish for approx. 25 minutes at 200°C, 400°F, Gas Mark 6. Serve hot.

 # Corn Pasta with Roasted Vegetables

1 garlic clove
75ml (5 tbsp) extra virgin
*   olive oil*
2 onions or some spring onions
6 tomatoes or a punnet of
*   cherry tomatoes*
6 courgettes
275g (10 oz) corn pasta spirals

A few basil leaves
50g (2 oz) pine kernels
Salt and black pepper
*   to taste*
50g (2 oz) 'Parmazano',
*   hard goats' cheese or*
*   hard sheep's cheese, grated*

Crush the garlic and mix with the olive oil. Cut the onion into wedges or spring onions into thick diagonal slices. Cut the tomatoes in wedges but leave the cherry tomatoes whole. Thickly slice the courgettes. Coat the vegetables with the garlic flavoured oil. Place the onion wedges and sliced courgettes in a large roasting tin and roast at 200°C, 400°F, Gas Mark 6 for 15 minutes. Remove from oven and turn the vegetables over. Add the tomato wedges or whole cherry tomatoes and the spring onions, if using. Return to oven for a further 15 minutes or until the vegetables are tender. Meanwhile, cook the corn pasta according to the instructions on the pack, taking care not to overcook it, and drain well. Toss together pasta, roasted vegetables along with the flavoured oil in the roasting tin, torn basil leaves and pine kernels. Garnish with 'Parmazano' or grated goats' or sheep's cheese and serve immediately.

C Use goats' cheese or sheep's cheese.

Spaghetti Neapolitan

60ml (4 tbsp) olive oil
2 onions, peeled and
  chopped
1 clove garlic, peeled and
  crushed
900g (2 lb) tomatoes,
  skinned and deseeded
60ml (4 tbsp) tomato
  purée
6 courgettes, sliced

225g (8 oz) gluten-free
  spaghetti, corn spaghetti
  or rice spaghetti
10–20ml (2–4 tsp) fresh
  basil, finely shredded
Salt and pepper to taste
Garnish:
Hard goats' cheese or
  hard sheep's cheese,
  grated or 'Parmazano'

Heat oil in pan, add onion and garlic and fry gently to soften. Remove with a slotted spoon. Add courgettes and fry until just brown. Return onion to pan together with tomatoes and tomato purée. Cook for a further 10 minutes, stirring occasionally, adding a little water, as necessary, to prevent the mixture from becoming too dry. Meanwhile, cook the spaghetti as directed on the packet, taking care not to overcook it. When vegetable mixture is ready, stir in the basil and season to taste. Serve vegetable sauce on a bed of spaghetti and garnish with grated cheese of choice or 'Parmazano'.

C Use goats' cheese or sheep's cheese.

 # Pasta with Vegetables in Tomato Sauce

60ml (4 tbsp) olive oil
1 garlic clove, crushed
2 leeks, sliced
400g (14 oz) can chopped
  tomatoes
225g (8 oz) broad beans
1 bay leaf

Salt and pepper to taste
400g (14 oz) can
  artichoke hearts
16 pitted black olives
275g (10 oz) corn pasta,
  rice and millet pasta,
  or buckwheat pasta
Sprigs of basil

Heat olive oil in a large pan and sauté garlic and leeks until softened. Add tomatoes, broad beans, bay leaf and seasoning.

Bring to the boil and simmer for 15 minutes. Remove bay leaf. Add the artichoke hearts, cut into chunks and the olives to the sauce and continue to cook for a further 5 minutes. Meanwhile, prepare the pasta according to the manufacturers' instructions, taking care not to overcook it. Add well-drained pasta to the sauce and mix. Garnish with sprigs of basil.

C̲ Use black olives in brine.
G̲r̲ Use buckwheat pasta.

C̲ E̲ Leek and Bean Savoury
G̲l̲ G̲r̲

225g (8 oz) flageolet beans
225g (8 oz) broccoli florets
450g (1 lb) leeks
40g (1½ oz) milk-free
   margarine
25g (1 oz) soya flour
300ml (½ pt) goats' milk,
   sheep's milk or soya milk

1 vegetable stock cube
Black pepper to taste

To serve:
225–250g (8–9 oz) 100%
   Soba, gluten-free
   spaghetti, corn spaghetti
   or rice spaghetti

Soak the beans overnight. Drain and place them in a pan of cold water, bring to the boil and cook for 45–50 minutes or until tender. Drain and set aside. Bring some water to the boil and cook the broccoli florets for 5–10 minutes, according to taste. Drain and set aside. Trim the leeks and cut diagonally into 1·5cm (½") slices. Meanwhile, cook the spaghetti as directed on the packet. Melt the margarine in a pan and sauté the leeks gently until tender. Stir in the soya flour and cook, stirring continuously, for 1 minute. Remove from the heat and gradually blend in the milk. Add the vegetable stock cube and sufficient water to make a sauce. Stir until stock cube is dissolved. Add the cooked beans and broccoli florets and season to taste with black pepper. Heat through gently. Place cooked spaghetti in a ring on each plate and pour the bean and leek sauce into the centre.

C̲ Use 'Kallo Yeast-free Vegetable Stock Cube'.
G̲r̲ Use 100% Soba (buckwheat noodles).

C E Gl Gr **Pasta and Pesto**

275g (10 oz) corn spaghetti,
  rice spaghetti, corn pasta,
  rice and millet pasta,
  buckwheat pasta or
  lentil pasta shells
25g (1 oz) fresh basil leaves
50g (2 oz) pine kernels
Salt and pepper to taste

2 garlic cloves, crushed
100ml (3½ fl oz) extra
  virgin olive oil
60ml (4 tbsp) 'Parmazano',
  hard goats' cheese or
  hard sheep's cheese, grated
Extra pine kernels to garnish

Cook pasta according to instructions on the pack, taking care not to overcook it. Meanwhile, place basil, pine kernels and garlic in a blender or food processor and blend until finely chopped. Add oil in a thin, steady stream with the machine running and the sauce will become creamy. Drain pasta, add sauce and toss well. Serve sprinkled with 'Parmazano' or grated cheese and extra pine kernels.

C Use goats' cheese or sheep's cheese.
Gr Use buckwheat pasta or lentil pasta shells.

□ E Gl Gr **Pizza**

Dough:
Use one batch of either 'Mixed Flour Bread' (see page 29), 'Potato and Rice Bread' (see page 27) or 'Potato and Buckwheat Bread' (see page 28).

Topping:
200ml (7 fl oz) thick
  tomato sauce
115g (4 oz) tomatoes,
  skinned and sliced
  or 2 red peppers, cut into
  halves and deseeded
115g (4 oz) hard goats'
  cheese or hard sheep's
  cheese, grated

115g (4 oz) mushrooms,
  sliced and sautéed or
  150g (5 oz) canned
  artichoke hearts,
  drained and halved
30–45ml (2–3 tbsp) olive oil
A few basil leaves
Black olives in brine

Divide dough between two greased or oiled sandwich tins and bake at 180°C, 350°F, Gas Mark 4 for 20 minutes. Meanwhile, if using red pepper, prepare by roasting skin side up until charred. Then remove the skin and slice the flesh. Spread each pizza base with thick tomato sauce and then place sliced tomato or red pepper and mushrooms or artichoke hearts on top. Sprinkle with olive oil. Finally, scatter with grated cheese, torn basil leaves and black olives. Return to oven for a further 15–20 minutes. Serve hot with salad.

Alternative:
These Pizza Bases can also be used as a substitute for Pitta Bread.

 Use Potato and Buckwheat dough.

Pan-fried Pizza

225g (8 oz) rye flour
1·25ml (¼ tsp) bicarbonate
  of soda

30ml (2 tbsp) oil of choice
150ml (¼ pt) cold water
Salt and pepper

Place all ingredients in a bowl and mix to a dough. Divide the dough into two and place on a floured board. Roll into rounds to fit the base of your frying pan. Heat a little oil in the pan, add one pizza base and cook until golden brown and then turn and cook other side. Transfer to grill pan or baking sheet. Cook other pizza base. Cover with topping as for previous recipe or topping of choice. Place under preheated grill until cheese is bubbling and golden.

Scone Pizza

150g (5 oz) brown rice flour
150g (5 oz) potato flour
5ml (1 tsp) bicarbonate of soda
1 egg

Pinch of salt
15ml (1 tbsp) olive oil
200ml (7 fl oz) goats' milk,
  sheep's milk or soya milk

Grease and flour two 20–23cm (8–9") sandwich tins. Place all ingredients in a bowl and mix well to a thick batter. Divide batter between the two tins and bake at 190°C, 375°F, Gas Mark 5 for 15 minutes. Cover with topping as for previous two recipes and place under preheated grill until cheese is bubbling and golden or return to oven and bake at 180°C, 350°F, Gas Mark 4 for 15–20 minutes.

Curry Sauce

1 onion, chopped
1 garlic clove, crushed
1 cooking apple, diced
25g (1 oz) root ginger, finely chopped or grated
75ml (3 fl oz) oil of choice
30ml (2 tbsp) curry powder
30ml (2 tbsp) cornflour or arrowroot
Salt and pepper to taste

15ml (1 tbsp) concentrated tomato or mushroom purée
50g (2 oz) natural sultanas (optional)
300ml (½ pt) tinned coconut milk
300ml (½ pt) vegetable stock
5ml (1 tsp) lemon juice

Gently sauté the onion, garlic, apple and ginger in the oil until onion is tender and transparent. Add curry powder and cornflour or arrowroot. Stir until blended and cook for a few minutes. Blend in tomato or mushroom purée. Add natural sultanas, tinned coconut milk and vegetable stock. Bring to the boil, stirring all the time. Cover and simmer for ¾ hour, remove lid and, if sauce is too thin, continue to cook with the lid off until sauce is sufficiently reduced. Stir in lemon juice and season to taste.

Alternative to tinned coconut milk:
115g (4 oz) creamed coconut, grated and mixed with 300ml (½ pt) goats' milk or sheep's milk.

Gr Use arrowroot.

Vegetable Curry

1 quantity 'Curry Sauce' (see above)

675g (1½ lb) assorted vegetables, chopped

Add the vegetables to the hot curry sauce after half an hour of cooking time and continue to cook until the vegetables are tender. Serve on a bed of boiled long-grain brown rice.

See Dietary Notes for 'Curry Sauce'.

 ## Nut and Pasta Curry

*225–250g (8–9 oz) gluten-
 free macaroni, corn pasta
 spirals, rice and millet
 pasta, buckwheat pasta
 or lentil pasta shells*

*175g (6 oz) cashews or
 walnuts, coarsely
 chopped*
*1 quantity 'Curry Sauce'
 (see page 159)*

Cook the pasta in boiling water, as directed on packet. Drain. Add with nuts to hot curry sauce and reheat gently. Pile onto warmed plates and serve with a side salad.

Gr Use buckwheat pasta spirals or legume pasta shells.
See Dietary Notes for 'Curry Sauce'.

 ## Egg and Pasta Curry

Follow recipe and method for 'Nut and Pasta Curry' substituting 4 large chopped boiled eggs for nuts.

See Dietary Notes for 'Curry Sauce' and 'Nut and Pasta Curry'.

 ## Lentil Curry

*225g (8 oz) lentils
2 large onions, chopped
1 small apple, peeled, cored
 and chopped
50g (2 oz) milk-free
 margarine or
 vegetable fat
15ml (1 tbsp) curry powder*

*5ml (1 tsp) muscovado
 sugar
Salt and pepper to taste
A little lemon juice
225g (8 oz) mixed vegetables
 of choice, diced and
 cooked*

Soak lentils overnight. Drain. Put into a saucepan and cover with fresh water, then bring to the boil. Simmer gently until just soft but still whole. Fry the onion and apple in fat until onion is transparent. Stir in curry powder and cook for 1 minute. Mix in all the other ingredients and simmer gently for a few minutes. Serve hot on a bed of boiled long-grain brown rice, buckwheat pasta spirals or lentil pasta shells.

Gr Serve with buckwheat pasta spirals or lentil pasta shells.

Bean Curry

Follow recipe and method for 'Lentil Curry', substituting any dried beans for lentils.

Gr Serve with buckwheat or lentil pasta.

Accompaniments for Curry

'Chutney' (see pages 180-1), toasted chopped nuts, finely chopped crystallised or stem ginger, 'Piccalilli' (see page 183), mandarin oranges, crushed pineapple, sieved hard-boiled eggs, 'Fried Onion Rings' (see below), Puppodums (made with chick pea [gram] flour) and 'Mint and Yoghurt Dressing' (see page 176).

Fried Onion Rings

50g (2 oz) chick pea flour   *Pinch of salt*
2·5ml (½ tsp) garam masala   *1 large onion*
50ml (2 fl oz) water

Place flour, garam masala and salt in a mixing bowl, add water and mix to a smooth batter. Season to taste. Leave to stand for 30 minutes. Peel a large onion and cut into 0·75cm (¼") slices. Separate into rings. Stir onion rings into batter and coat well. Fry in deep hot fat or oil, cooking a few at a time, until golden and crisp. Drain well on crumpled kitchen paper. Keep hot.

Vegetarian 'Sausage' and Apple Pie

175g (6 oz) brown rice flour
30ml (2 tsp) gluten-free
  baking powder
Pinch of salt
75g (3 oz) vegetable
  shortening
175g (6 oz) cooked
  potato, sieved
3 medium-sized cooking
  apples

15ml (1 tbsp) fresh
  parsley, chopped
225g (8 oz) cooked green
  lentils, well drained
15ml (1 tbsp) concentrated
  tomato, vegetable or
  mushroom purée
15ml (1 tbsp) onion, grated
5ml (1 tsp) fresh thyme or
  sage, finely chopped
Salt and pepper to taste

Sieve flour, baking powder and salt into a bowl. Rub in the vegetable shortening until the mixture resembles fine breadcrumbs. Add sieved potato and mix in using the fingers to draw the mixture together, adding a little water if necessary. Knead lightly and set aside. Peel, core and slice apples and mix with the chopped parsley. Arrange in base of greased 750ml (1½ pt) deep Pyrex pie plate. Add purée of choice to cooked lentils and beat until smooth. Stir in the grated onion, thyme or sage and seasoning. Spread this mixture over apples. Roll out the pie crust and lift gently into place, trim and knock up the edge. Bake at 200°C, 400°F, Gas Mark 6 for 25–30 minutes or until cooked and top is golden brown. Serve hot.

Chestnut and Egg Deep Pie

Double quantity Pastry
  (see pages 85 or 86)
225g (8 oz) fresh chestnuts
  or 200g (7 oz) vacuum-
  packed whole chestnuts
1 quantity Lentil Savoury
  Mix, Haricot Bean Savoury
  Mix or Yellow Pea Savoury
  Mix (see pages 148–150)

2·5ml (½ tsp) dried sage
15ml (1 tbsp) lemon juice
Salt and pepper
Black olives in brine
5 hard boiled eggs,
  shelled
Beaten egg, to glaze

To prepare fresh chestnuts:
Nick the shells with a pair of scissors and then blanch in boiling water for 5 minutes. Remove with a slotted spoon. Peel off the outer skin and while still hot rub off the inner skin with a cloth. Boil for 40 minutes. Drain.
Line a deep cake tin with two thirds of the pastry. Stir the dried sage and the lemon juice into the savoury mix. Put one third of this mixture into pastry base and smooth out. Arrange drained black olives in a layer, add the 5 whole shelled eggs in a ring, pack the prepared chestnuts around the eggs and then cover with the rest of the savoury mix. Cover with a pastry lid and make a hole in the centre for the steam to come out. Brush the top with beaten egg. Bake at 200°C, 400°F, Gas Mark 6 for 40–50 minutes or until pastry top is nicely browned. Serve hot with brussel sprouts or fennel and roast potatoes or serve cold with a salad.

C Use *'Kallo Yeast-free Vegetable Stock Cubes'*, yeast-free
    breadcrumbs and omit lemon juice, if not allowed.
Gl Use gluten-free pastry of choice.
Gr Use grain-free pastry of choice.

Walnut Flan

Line a 20–23cm (8–9") flan tin with pastry of choice (see pages 84-86).

Filling:

2 onions, chopped
1 clove garlic, crushed
15ml (1 tbsp) oil of choice
350g (12 oz) walnuts,
  ground
2 eggs, beaten
2·5ml (½ tsp) fresh thyme

5ml (1 tsp) tomato or
  mushroom purée
50g (2 oz) plain breadcrumbs
  or soda breadcrumbs, any
  type (see pages 26–42)
25g (1 oz) milk-free
  margarine

Fry onion and garlic in oil until transparent. Add nuts, beaten eggs, herbs and purée. Mix well and then spoon mixture into prepared flan case, sprinkling the breadcrumbs on the top. Dot with margarine. Bake at 200°C, 400°F, Gas Mark 6 for about 30 minutes. Serve hot with roast potatoes, vegetables and cranberry

sauce or cold with salad.
If serving cold can be glazed as follows:
Drain a small tin of pineapple rings in natural juice and decorate top of flan. Coat with Savoury Aspic (see page 165).

C Use soda breadcrumbs of choice and tomato purée.
Gl Use gluten-free pastry and breadcrumbs of choice.
Gr Use grain-free pastry and breadcrumbs of choice.

CE Gl Sweetcorn and Tofu Flan

Line a 20cm (8") flan tin with pastry of choice (see pages 84-86).

Filling:

150g (5 oz) sweetcorn	*5ml (1 tsp) oil of choice*
115g (4 oz) onion or leek	*225g (8 oz) tofu, mashed*
1 large garlic clove	*Salt and pepper to taste*

Cook the sweetcorn kernels until tender and drain. Bake the pastry case 'blind' for 10 minutes at 200°C, 400°F, Gas Mark 6. Chop onion or leek and crush garlic. Heat oil in a frying pan and cook onion or leek and garlic for about 7 minutes over gentle heat. Remove from heat, mix in tofu thoroughly, adding a little water to make a slightly soft consistency. Season with salt and black pepper to taste. Add cooked sweetcorn and stir well. Spoon into part-baked flan case and bake at 190°C, 375°F, Gas Mark 5 for 25 minutes.

Gl Use gluten-free pastry of choice.

C Gl Gr Soya Savoury Loaf

225g (8 oz) textured soya	*A little soya oil*
* protein*	*225ml (8 fl oz) soya milk*
450ml (16 fl oz) water	*5ml (1 tsp) yeast or*
1 medium onion, chopped	* vegetable extract*
50g (2 oz) plain breadcrumbs	*1·25ml (¼ tsp) dried sage*
* or soda breadcrumbs, any*	*Salt and pepper to taste*
* type (see pages 26-42)*	*2 eggs*

Put textured soya protein and water into a saucepan and simmer to soften. Fry the chopped onion in the oil until transparent. Combine all the ingredients well and place in an oiled ovenproof loaf dish. Bake at 180°C, 350°F, Gas Mark 4 for 1 hour. Serve hot or cold.

C Use soda breadcrumbs of choice and vegetable extract.
Gl Use gluten-free breadcrumbs of choice.
Gr Use grain-free breadcrumbs of choice.

C E Gl Gr Savoury Aspic

15ml (3 tsp) gelatine
or 7·5ml (1½ tsp)
agar agar
60ml (4 tbsp) hot water
Pinch of salt

300ml (½ pt) well-flavoured
clear vegetable stock
30ml (2 tbsp) cider vinegar
(preservative-free),
brown rice vinegar
or lemon juice

Dissolve the gelatine or agar agar in hot water, according to the manufacturers' instructions, and add to stock. Add vinegar or lemon juice. Leave until just beginning to thicken and use as required.

C Use lemon juice, if allowed, and ½ a 'Kallo Yeast-free Vegetable Stock Cube'.
Gr Use cider vinegar or lemon juice.

C E Gl Gr Tomato Aspic

15ml (3 tsp) gelatine
or 7·5ml (1½ tsp)
agar agar
150ml (¼ pt) hot water
300ml (½ pt) tomato juice
1 slice of onion
Salt and pepper to taste

5ml (1 tsp) sugar or
2·5ml (½ tsp) fructose
(optional)
15ml (1 tbsp) cider vinegar
(preservative-free),
brown rice vinegar or
lemon juice

Put the gelatine or agar agar in the hot water to dissolve, according to the manufacturers' instructions. Add all flavourings to half of the tomato juice and cook until onion softens. Stir in the dissolved gelatine or agar agar and then add the rest of the ingredients. Strain and leave until just beginning to thicken and use as required.

C Use lemon juice, if allowed, and omit sugar.
Gr Use cider vinegar or lemon juice.

C E Gl Gr Moulded Vegetable Salad

Choose a variety of vegetables of different colours. Here are some suggestions: cooked peas, lightly cooked green beans, diced celery, cooked diced carrot, diced cucumber, diced cooked beetroot, small pieces of green or red pepper, finely chopped onion, asparagus tips, or sliced radishes.

1 quantity 'Savoury Aspic' or   *½ cup each of 4 or 5 different*
   'Tomato Aspic' (see above)   *vegetables*

Prepare aspic and let it cool. Pour a little into the bottom of a plain mould and chill. When set, place pieces of vegetable onto the gel to form a pattern or design. Repeat the process also on each side of the mould, if wished. Chill until set. Fill mould with rest of vegetables and then carefully pour in rest of aspic. Chill until firmly set. Unmould onto a bed of lettuce and serve.

See Dietary Notes given for 'Savoury Aspic' or 'Tomato Aspic'.

Soya and Nut Moulds

10ml (2 tsp) soya flour   *150ml (¼ pt) soya milk*
300ml (½ pt) water   *A little tamari*
20ml (4 tsp) gelatine or   *115g (4 oz) nuts of choice,*
*   10ml (2 tsp) agar agar*   *   ground or grated*

Whisk flour and water together and then bring to the boil. Cook for a minute or two and then allow to cool. Dissolve the gelatine or agar agar in a little hot water, according to the manufacturers' instructions. Add the soya milk and the soya flour mixture. Make up to 575ml (1 pt) with cold water. Flavour with tamari and leave until just starting to set. Stir in the prepared nuts and pour into wetted individual moulds and leave to set. Turn out of moulds and serve on a bed of salad.

C E GI Savoury Millet Blancmange

575ml (1 pt) goats' milk,
  sheep's milk or soya milk
2·5ml (½ tsp) celery salt
60ml (4 tbsp) millet flakes
15ml (1 tbsp) fresh parsley,
  finely chopped

A little chopped chives
2·5ml (½ tsp) fresh thyme,
  finely chopped
60ml (4 tbsp) hard goats'
  cheese, hard sheep's
  cheese or soya cheese,
  grated

Put the milk, celery salt and flakes in a pan and bring to the boil. Boil for 10 minutes. Stir in the other ingredients and pour into a rinsed mould and leave to set. Serve on a large dish surrounded by salad.

Alternatives:
The herbs and cheese are only a suggestion. You can use whatever you wish, e.g. sautéed mushrooms with oregano or tomato with basil.

C Use goats' cheese or sheep's cheese.

Salads and Dressings

⬚ Carrot and Celeriac Salad

15ml (1 tbsp) lemon juice
15ml (1 tbsp) fresh parsley,
  finely chopped
15ml (1 tbsp) extra virgin
  olive oil

150g (5 oz) goats' yoghurt
  or sheep's yoghurt
Salt and pepper to taste
225g (8 oz) carrots
350g (12 oz) celeriac

Make the dressing first by mixing together lemon juice, parsley, olive oil and yoghurt and then season to taste. Grate the carrot and celeriac into a bowl, add the yoghurt dressing and toss well. Garnish with a sprig of parsley and serve immediately.

C Use lemon, if allowed.

Apple and Celery Salad

2 eating apples
1 head of celery

1 quantity 'Yoghurt Dressing'
or 'French Dressing'
(see page 175)

Dice apple and slice celery. Put into a bowl. Add chilled dressing and toss well. Serve immediately.

 # Cucumber Salad

1 quantity 'Spring Onion
and Yoghurt Dressing' or
'Soya Mayonnaise' (see
pages 175 & 178)

2·5ml (½ tsp) fresh
tarragon, chopped
1 cucumber, diced
Salt and pepper to taste

Combine the tarragon and dressing. Add diced unpeeled cucumber and toss. Season to taste. Cover and chill until required. Keeps for 2 days in the refrigerator.

 # Creamy Beetroot Salad

120ml (8 tbsp) 'Soya
Mayonnaise' (see page 178)

225g (8oz) raw beetroot,
grated

Mix the raw beetroot with the dressing. Chill and serve.

 # Mustard Family Salad

1 head chinese leaves or
½ white cabbage
Bunch of watercress
Box of mustard and cress
Rocket leaves

Radishes
Tiny cauliflower florets
'Mustard & Yoghurt
Dressing' or 'Mustard
Mayonnaise' (see pages
176 & 178)

Cut chinese leaves into 2·5cm (1") strips or finely shred white cabbage. Place chinese leaves or cabbage on serving dish and arrange mixture of the other leaves on top. Cut radishes into flowers. Garnish salad with radish flowers and cauliflower florets. Serve dressing or mayonnaise in a separate bowl.

C Use 'Yoghurt Dressing' or 'Soya Mayonnaise' (see pages 175 and 178).
E Use 'Mustard & Yoghurt Dressing'.

[C][E][Gl][Gr] Mixed Bean Salad

Mix together a variety of dried beans of mixed colours and soak overnight. Rinse. Cook in fresh water until all varieties are tender. Drain and leave until completely cold. Toss with a little soya oil.

[C][E][Gl][Gr] Coconut Coleslaw

*1 quantity 'Spring Onion and
  Yoghurt Dressing' or 'Soya
  Mayonnaise' (see pages
  (176 & 178)
½ white cabbage, shredded*

*75g (3 oz) unsulphured
  desiccated coconut
Pinch of paprika or
  mild curry powder
Spring onions for garnish*

Soak coconut in dressing or salad cream for ½ hour. Add rest of ingredients and place in a serving dish. Garnish with chopped spring onions.

[C][E][Gl][Gr] Sweet Potato Salad

*120ml (8 tbsp) 'Soya
  Mayonnaise' (see page 178)*

*225g (8 oz) sweet potatoes
  (white fleshed)*

Gently wash the sweet potatoes and cook in boiling salted water until just tender. Drain and leave until cold. Remove skins and dice the sweet potatoes and combine with the mayonnaise. Chill and serve.

Tangy Pepper Salad

1 red pepper
1 green pepper
2 oranges
Lettuce

60ml (4 tbsp) 'Honey and
Lemon Dressing' (see
page 175)

Shred the peppers, after removing the seeds and the pith. Cut the peel from the oranges, removing all the white pith, and divide into segments by cutting each segment free from skin. Toss peppers and oranges with the Honey and Lemon Dressing and arrange on prepared bed of lettuce.

 ## Rice Medley

150g (5 oz) long-grain
brown rice, cooked
75g (3 oz) wild rice, cooked
25g (1 oz) natural raisins
8 spring onions, chopped
Salt and pepper to taste

25g (1 oz) hazelnuts, flaked
25g (1 oz) sunflower seeds
15ml (1 tbsp) fresh parsley,
chopped
Stuffed green olives in brine,
halved

Place all ingredients, except the olives, in a salad bowl and mix. Garnish with the halved stuffed olives.

Russian Salad

115g (4 oz) green beans,
lightly cooked and chilled
175g (6 oz) potatoes,
cooked and chilled
175g (6 oz) carrots,
cooked and chilled
½ medium cauliflower,
lightly cooked and chilled
4 sticks celery

4 gherkins
5ml (1 tsp) fresh chives,
chopped
Salt and pepper to taste
300ml (½ pt) 'Mayonnaise'
or 'Soya Mayonnaise' (see
pages 177 & 178)
Lettuce

Slice beans and dice potato and carrot. Cut cauliflower into small florets. Chop celery and slice gherkins. Put all the vegetables into a large bowl. Add half the chopped chives, seasoning and mayonnaise. Toss gently so as not to break the vegetables. Pile onto a bed of lettuce and top with remaining chopped chives.

C Omit gerkins and use 'Soya Mayonnaise'.
E Use 'Soya Mayonnaise'.

C E Gl Gr Belgian Salad

60ml (4 tbsp) olive oil
Juice of 1 lemon
Salt and pepper to taste
Small bunch of dill
3 heads of chicory

175g (6 oz) carrot
6 radishes
50g (2 oz) walnuts or
   pecans, shelled
1 eating apple

Beat together the oil, ½ the lemon juice, salt and pepper. Chop the dill finely, reserving a few sprigs for garnish. Arrange chicory leaves around the edge of a large flat dish, radiating out from the centre. Slice remaining chicory leaves. Peel carrot and cut into julienne strips or grate. Trim and slice radishes. Cut walnuts or pecans in half. Dice apple and place in a large bowl and coat with remaining lemon juice; drain off surplus. Add the rest of the prepared vegetables and the nuts. Toss together with the dressing and chopped dill. Pile in centre of dish with the chicory leaves showing all the way round. Garnish with reserved sprigs of dill.

C Use ½ of the lemon, if allowed, and omit apple.

C E Gl Gr Frankfurter Salad

10 vegetarian sausages
   (wheat-free)
2 eggs
225g (8 oz) white cabbage
2 carrots
2 sticks celery

8 radishes
1 red-skinned apple
90ml (6 tbsp) 'Mayonnaise'
   or 'Soya Mayonnaise' (see
   pages 177 & 178)

Prepare the vegetarian sausages according to instructions on pack and leave until cold. Hard-boil eggs for 10 minutes, crack and leave in cold water until cold. Shell, dry the eggs and then cut into wedges. Shred the cabbage. Peel and grate carrot and slice the celery and radishes. Quarter, core and dice the unpeeled apple. Place the apple in large bowl and mix with mayonnaise straight away to prevent it going brown. Cut sausages into 1·25cm (½") pieces. Place all ingredients except egg into the bowl and mix well. Finally add egg and mix gently. Chill until ready to serve.

C Use 'Soya Mayonnaise' and omit apple.
E Omit eggs.
Gl Use gluten-free vegetarian sausages.
Gr Use grain-free vegetarian sausages.

 # Tuscan Bean Salad

A colourful salad that is quick to make. Any tinned beans could be used to ring the changes.

Small radicchio
3 hard-boiled eggs
425g (15 oz) tinned cannellini
  beans
200g (7 oz) tinned butter beans
1 small red onion
25g (1 oz) black olives, stoned

45ml (3 tbsp) extra virgin
  olive oil
30ml (2 tbsp) lemon juice
2 sticks celery
Salt and pepper to taste
15ml (1 tbsp) fresh parsley
  in tiny sprigs

Arrange the radicchio leaves on 4 individual plates. Cut the eggs into wedges and set aside. Drain the beans and then rinse and drain again. Place them in a large bowl together with finely sliced onion, olives, olive oil, lemon juice and finely sliced celery. Season with salt and pepper and mix. Add the egg wedges carefully so as not to break them. Spoon the mixture over the radicchio and garnish with sprigs of parsley.

C Use sugar-free tinned beans and black olives in brine. Omit lemon juice if not allowed.

Parsleyed Leeks and Mushrooms

6 leeks
Salt
175g (6 oz) button
  mushrooms
1 garlic clove, crushed
75ml (5 tbsp) oil of choice

10ml (2 tsp) sugar
15ml (1 tbsp) cider vinegar
  (preservative-free)
  or brown rice vinegar
Black pepper to taste
30ml (2 tbsp) fresh
  parsley, chopped

Trim leeks and cut diagonally into 5cm (2") pieces. Cook in boiling salted water for 8–10 minutes or until only just tender. Clean mushrooms and thinly slice. Lightly sauté the garlic and mushrooms in 15ml (1 tbsp) of the oil. Place the sugar, vinegar and the remaining oil in a small bowl and season with black pepper. Mix well and stir in chopped parsley. Lightly toss hot drained leeks and sliced mushrooms in prepared parsley dressing. Leave to cool, turning the ingredients occasionally. Serve cold.

Gr Use cider vinegar.

Melon Salad

½ large or 1 small honeydew
  melon
50g (2 oz) natural seedless
  raisins
5ml (1 tsp) spring onion,
  finely chopped
50g (2 oz) almonds, flaked
45ml (3 tbsp) 'French Dressing'
  (see page 175)

15ml (1 tsp) 'Grey Poupon
  Dijon Mustard' or
  Mustard (see page 183)
30ml (2 tbsp) goats' yoghurt
  or sheep's yoghurt
30ml (2 tbsp) fresh
  parsley, chopped
To serve: Chinese leaves

Cut the flesh out of the melon and dice. Place in a bowl with raisins, spring onion and almonds. Blend dressing with mustard, yoghurt and parsley. Pour over melon mixture and toss lightly. Serve on a bed of Chinese leaves.

French Dressing

20ml (4 tsp) cider vinegar
   (preservative-free),
   brown rice vinegar or
   lemon juice

45ml (3 tbsp) extra virgin
   olive oil
Salt and pepper to taste

Put ingredients into a screw-topped jar and shake well to blend.

C Use lemon juice, if allowed.
Gr Use cider vinegar or lemon juice.

Honey and Lemon Dressing

15ml (1 tbsp) sunflower oil
15ml (1 tbsp) lemon juice

15ml (1 tbsp) clear honey

Put ingredients into a screw-topped jar and shake well to blend.

Yoghurt Dressing

45ml (3 tbsp) goats' yoghurt
   or sheep's yoghurt
30ml (2 tbsp) extra virgin
   olive oil

15ml (1 tbsp) lemon juice
Pinch of paprika or
   celery salt (optional)

Put all ingredients into a bowl and mix very well. Use straight away.

C Use lemon, if allowed lemon.

Mint and Yoghurt Dressing

Follow recipe and method for 'Yoghurt Dressing'. Add 15ml (1 tbsp) chopped mint (or according to taste) and omit paprika or celery salt. Season with salt, if desired. This dressing makes a good accompaniment for curry dishes.

C If allowed lemon.

Spring Onion and Yoghurt Dressing

Follow recipe and method for 'Yoghurt Dressing'. Add 15ml (1 tbsp) finely chopped spring onion and omit the paprika or celery salt. Season with salt, if desired.

C If allowed lemon.

Mustard and Yoghurt Dressing

Follow recipe and method for 'Yoghurt Dressing'. Add 7·5ml (½ tbsp) *'Grey Poupon Dijon Mustard'* or 'Mustard' (see page 183) according to taste and omit paprika or celery salt. Season with salt, if desired.

Tarragon Dressing

Zest of 1 lemon
150ml (¼ pt) 'Mayonnaise'
    (see next page)

30ml (2 tbsp) fresh
    tarragon, chopped

Mix zest with the mayonnaise. Add the chopped tarragon and mix well.

Nut Butter Dressing

45ml (3 tbsp) 'Nut Butter'
(see page 187)
15ml (1 tbsp) lemon juice
80ml (3 fl oz) cold water

15ml (1 tbsp) 'Grey Poupon
Dijon Mustard' or
'Mustard' (see page 183)
Salt and pepper to taste

Put all ingredients in a screw-topped jar and shake well until completely blended.

 # Egg-free Salad Cream

50g (2 oz) milk-free
margarine
10ml (2 tsp) fructose
5ml (1 tsp) cider vinegar
(preservative-free)
or brown rice vinegar

20ml (4 tsp) water
5ml (1 tsp) oil of choice
Squeeze of lemon juice
Salt and pepper to taste

Put margarine and fructose in a bowl and beat with a wooden spoon until creamy. Beat in vinegar of choice a little at a time and then do the same with the water and the oil. Finally beat in the lemon juice and seasoning. Put in a jar with a wide neck and a screw top. Store in the refrigerator.

Gr Use cider vinegar.

 # Mayonnaise

1 egg yolk
5ml (1 tsp) honey
Pinch of salt

Juice of ½ lemon
300ml (½ pt) olive oil

Put egg yolk, honey, salt and lemon juice into liquidiser and blend briefly. Remove the porthole lid in the top of the liquidiser and gradually pour in oil, incorporating all the while, until the mayonnaise is thick. Put in a jar with a wide neck and a screw top. Store in the refrigerator.

CE / GlGr Soya Mayonnaise

25g (1 oz) soya flour	Pinch of salt
30ml (2 tbsp) water	Juice of ½ lemon or 15ml
225ml (8 fl oz) soya oil	(1 tbsp) cider vinegar
	(preservative-free)

Make a smooth paste of soya flour and water in a bowl, standing in a pan of hot water, and let it heat. Slowly beat in oil with a rotary beater. Remove from heat when thick, season and add lemon juice or cider vinegar. Beat until smooth and thick. Put in a jar with a wide neck and a screw top. Store in the refrigerator.

C Use lemon juice if allowed.

Mustard Mayonnaise

1 egg	10ml (2 tsp) brown rice
2·5ml (½ tsp) salt	vinegar
7·5–15ml (½–1 tbsp) 'Grey	300ml (½ pt) rapeseed or
Poupon Dijon Mustard' or	corn oil
'Mustard' (see page 183)	

To make the mayonnaise using a liquidiser:
Break the egg into the liquidiser, add the salt, mustard (according to taste) and vinegar. Blend for 10 seconds. While the liquidiser is switched on, slowly pour in the oil through the port-hole in the lid. The mayonnaise will become thick as the oil is added.
To make the mayonnaise by hand:
Beat the egg, salt, mustard and vinegar together with a wooden spoon. Add the oil a little at a time until half of the oil has been used. Then using more of the oil at each addition, continue until all the rest of the oil has been blended in and the mayonnaise is thick and smooth.

Pistou

Pistou is similar to Pesto without the cheese and is used as a dressing for pasta.

50g (2 oz) fresh basil leaves
2 garlic cloves, skinned
30g (2 tbsp) pine kernels

115ml (4 fl oz) extra
virgin olive oil
Salt and pepper to taste

Place the basil, garlic, pine kernels and olive oil in a blender or food processor and blend at high speed until creamy. Season to taste. Store in a screw-topped jar in the fridge for up to 2 weeks.

 Pesto

This non-dairy version of Pesto is suitable for Vegans.

Follow recipe and method for 'Pistou' adding 50g (2 oz) 'Parmazano'.

Preserves, Savoury and Sweet

☐☐ **Apple Chutney**
GI Gr

900g (2 lb) apples, cored and
  peeled
450g (1 lb) natural seedless
  raisins
450g (1 lb) onions
25g (1 oz) mustard seeds,
  ground

450g (1 lb) demerara sugar
5ml (1 tsp) cayenne pepper
10ml (2 tsp) salt
1·125 litres (2 pt) brown rice
  vinegar or cider vinegar
  (preservative-free)

Chop apples, raisins (if large) and onion coarsely and mix with
the other ingredients. Stew until the chopped ingredients are
tender which will take about one hour. Pour into warm jars and
seal in the usual way.

Gr Use cider vinegar.

Apricot Chutney

900g (2 lb) unsulphured
   dried apricots
225g (8 oz) onions
1·350kg (3 lb) demerara
   sugar
5ml (1 tsp) curry powder

5ml (1 tsp) cinnamon
5ml (1 tsp) allspice
Pinch of cayenne pepper
1·125 litres (2 pt) brown
   rice vinegar or cider vinegar
   (preservative-free)

Wash the apricots well, cover them with boiling water and leave for 24 hours. Chop onions and stew them with a little of the sugar until tender. Drain the apricots, cut into pieces and put into the pan with the rest of the ingredients. Simmer until chutney is thick which will take about 2 hours. Pot and cover in the usual way.

Gr Use cider vinegar.

Prune Chutney

An unusual chutney without onion or tomato.

450g (1 lb) unsorbated prunes
350g (12 oz) apples
275g (10 oz) muscovado
   sugar
115g (4 oz) hazelnuts
Pinch of cayenne pepper

300ml (½ pt) brown rice
   vinegar or cider vinegar
   (preservative-free)
2·5ml (½ tsp) curry powder
2·5ml (½ tsp) cinnamon
Pinch of allspice

Pour boiling water over the prunes and leave for 24 hours. Peel and core the apples, chop finely and stew until tender with a little of the sugar. Chop nuts finely. Remove prune stones, and cut prunes into pieces. Put vinegar of choice into a pan, add the sugar and mix in the remaining ingredients. Boil for ¾–1 hour, stirring frequently. Pot and cover at once.

Gr Use cider vinegar.

Tomato Ketchup

1·350kg (3 lb) ripe tomatoes
50g (2 oz) salt
575ml (1 pt) cider vinegar
    (preservative-free)
    or brown rice vinegar

50g (2 oz) demerara sugar
10ml (2 tsp) mustard seeds,
    ground
5ml (1 tsp) white pepper

Put tomatoes into a large bowl and pour boiling water over them. Steep for a few minutes and then drain and peel. Chop them coarsely and sprinkle with salt. Leave for 3 hours. Add to pan with the rest of the ingredients and boil for ½ hour or until thick and smooth. Stir frequently while cooking to prevent mixture from sticking to the bottom of the pan. Pour into warm bottles while still hot and seal. When cold store in the refrigerator for short-term use. To store the ketchup for a longer time it is necessary to sterilise the filled and sealed bottles in boiling water for ½ hour. This can also be done in a pressure cooker by following the maker's instructions.

Gr Use cider vinegar.

 # Mushroom Ketchup

Makes a good alternative to the more traditional tomato ketchup.

1·350kg (3 lb) mushrooms
50g (2 oz) salt
15g (½ oz) fresh root ginger
575ml (1 pt) cider vinegar
    (preservative-free)
    or brown rice vinegar
5ml (1 tsp) allspice

1 blade of mace
6 cloves
½ stick of cinnamon
1 onion, finely chopped
2·5ml (½ tsp) horseradish,
    grated

Break the mushrooms into small pieces, sprinkle with salt and leave for 12 hours. Mash with a wooden spoon. Peel and coarsely chop the fresh root ginger. Put all ingredients into a pan, cover and simmer for ½ hour. Strain through a fine sieve and pour into warm jars or bottles, leaving a 4cm (1½") gap at the top for expansion. When cold store in the refrigerator for short-term use. To store the ketchup for a longer time it is necessary to sterilise the filled and sealed bottles in boiling water for ½ hour. This can also be done in a pressure cooker by following the maker's instructions.

Gr Use cider vinegar.

Piccalilli

1 large cauliflower
2 cucumbers
900g (2 lb) shallots or
pickling onions
900g (2 lb) apples
Brine
25g (1 oz) chilli peppers
50g (2 oz) garlic
25g (1 oz) root ginger, bruised

25g (1 oz) black peppercorns
2·2 litres (4 pt) brown rice
vinegar or cider vinegar
(preservative-free)
50g (2 oz) arrowroot or
cornflour
25g (1 oz) turmeric
25g (1 oz) mustard seeds,
ground

Prepare all the vegetables and apples and cut into neat pieces. Cover with cold brine, leave overnight and then drain. Prepare the pickle sauce by boiling the chilli peppers, garlic, ginger and peppercorns in the vinegar for 5 minutes, and then pour in the arrowroot or cornflour, turmeric and ground mustard seeds, which have previously been blended with a little cold vinegar. Stir and boil for 10 minutes to cook the starch. Pile the prepared vegetables into hot jars and pour over the pickling sauce. Cover and seal in the usual way.

Gr Use cider vinegar and arrowroot.

Mustard

The mustard seeds may be left whole or ground to a fine powder in a blender or pestle and mortar.

50g (2 oz) mustard seeds,
whole or ground
25g (1 oz) cornflour or
arrowroot
300ml (½ pt) cider vinegar
(preservative-free)

or brown rice vinegar
1 large pinch each of
ground ginger, ground
cloves and ground
caraway seeds
5ml (1 tsp) salt

Mix together the mustard, cornflour or arrowroot, spices and salt. Blend in the vinegar and cook gently until it forms a fairly thick paste. Allow to cool and store in small sealed pots.

Gr Use cider vinegar and arrowroot.

Mint Sauce Concentrate

To every 225g (8 oz) freshly picked mint leaves, allow 575ml (1pt) brown rice vinegar or cider vinegar and 450g (1 lb) sugar.

Wash and dry the leaves, chop finely and put in dry, wide-necked jars. Dissolve the sugar in the vinegar, stirring with a wooden spoon, allow to come to the boil and then leave to get cold. Pour over the chopped mint and seal the jars to make them airtight.
To prepare the sauce for the table:
Lift out sufficient mint with a wooden spoon, together with a little of the liquid. Put into a sauce boat and add sufficient fresh brown rice or cider vinegar to obtain the required consistency.

Gr Use cider vinegar.

Lemon Curd

2 large lemons
25g (1 oz) milk-free
 margarine

225g (8 oz) demerara sugar
2 eggs

Put the grated rind and juice from the lemons into a small basin together with the margarine and sugar. Stand the basin over a saucepan of boiling water. While this is getting hot, beat the eggs. Stir into the other ingredients and cook until thick; this takes about ½ hour. Pot and seal as for jam. Keeps very well.

Orange Curd

Follow the recipe and method for 'Lemon Curd' substituting the rind and juice of 2 oranges and the juice of 1 lemon for the 2 large lemons.

Dairy Substitutes

 ## Curd Cheese

*½ litre (1 pt) goats' milk
or sheep's milk*

22ml (1½ tbsp) lemon juice

Boil the milk and then stir in the lemon juice. Continue to boil for 1 minute until the curds separate. Leave to cool for 1 hour. Strain through muslin, and squeeze out all liquid. Tie up muslin and cover with cling-film, then press under heavy weights for several hours in the refrigerator. This makes a mild cheese which can be flavoured with chopped chives or other herbs of choice.

Keeps for 2 or 3 days in the refrigerator. This makes a small portion of cheese suitable for one person. For a family use 2·2 litres (4 pts) of milk of choice and 90ml (6 tbsp) lemon juice.

For a goats' cheese with a little more body add dried goats' milk at the rate of 30ml (2 tbsp) dried goats' milk to every ½ litre (1 pt) of fresh milk. Whisk the dried milk into the fresh milk before adding the lemon juice.

C If allowed lemon.

C E / Gl Gr Curd Cheese with Herbs

350g (12 oz) goats' or sheep's
  'Curd Cheese' (see above)
1 small clove garlic
Salt and pepper to taste
2·5ml (½ tsp) fresh basil,
  finely chopped

2·5ml (½ tsp) fresh thyme,
  finely chopped
15ml (1 tbsp) fresh parsley,
  finely chopped
4–6 bay leaves

Sieve curd cheese into a bowl. Using the blade of a knife crush the garlic with a little salt until very fine. Add to cheese along with rest of ingredients except the bay leaves. Mix well. Press into a small bowl or turn onto a damp board and form into a round cheese shape. Press bay leaves on top or around sides and leave for several hours for the flavour to mature. Remove bay leaves before serving with a choice of crispbreads.

C If allowed lemon.

Mock Cream

15ml (1 tbsp) arrowroot
75ml (5 tbsp) cold water

40g (1½ oz) milk-free
  margarine
Sweeten to taste

Place arrowroot in a saucepan and add water, stirring all the time. Heat and stir until the mixture thickens. Beat until smooth, then put in a basin and leave until completely cold. Add margarine and beat well. Sweeten to taste and continue to beat until fluffy. Use within 2 days.

Flavourings:
A few drops of orange or lemon juice, cocoa or carob powder, natural vanilla or a few drops of orange water or distilled rose water. Add at the final stage and beat well.

⊞ Nut Cream

115g (4 oz) cashews or
  blanched almonds
90ml (6 tbsp) water

A little honey or maple
  syrup, if desired

Grind nuts in blender to a fine powder. Add rest of ingredients and blend until smooth and creamy. Chill.
This cream has the consistency of evaporated milk.

C Omit sweetener.

⊞ Nut Butter

Any variety of nuts may be used. Spread the shelled nuts out on a baking tray and roast at 180°C, 350°F, Gas Mark 4 for anything up to 15 minutes, according to taste. Stir the nuts occasionally while they are roasting to ensure they are evenly done. Grind in liquidiser or blender by dropping a few nuts at a time onto the rotating blades through the porthole in the lid. Keep adding a little vegetable or nut oil of choice to make a paste and continue until contents are smooth. At the end of the process mix in a little salt to taste. The amount required is usually about 2·5ml (½ tsp) salt to 450g (1 lb) nuts. Put in a jar with a wide neck and screw top. Store in the refrigerator.

C̄|Ē Ḡl|Ḡr Nut Milk

115g (4 oz) cashews or   *15–30ml (1–2 tbsp)*
*   blanched almonds*   *   honey or maple syrup*
1·125 litres (2 pt) water   *   (according to taste)*

Grind nuts in liquidiser or blender to a fine powder. Add about 250ml (½ pt) water and the honey or maple syrup. Blend until smooth and then add rest of water and blend again. Chill.

C̄ Omit sweetener.

C̄|Ē Ḡl|Ḡr Coconut Cream

75g (3 oz) creamed coconut   *150ml (¼ pt) hot water*

Cut the creamed coconut into pieces and put into a bowl. Pour the hot water over it and beat until coconut has completely dispersed. Leave until cold.
This cream has the consistency of evaporated milk.

C̄|Ē Ḡl|Ḡr Coconut Milk

Follow recipe and method for 'Coconut Cream' adding up to 150ml (¼ pt) cold water after the coconut cream has been allowed to become cold.

C̄|Ē Ḡl|Ḡr Sunflower Seed Spread

225g (8 oz) sunflower seeds   *Salt (optional)*
115ml (4 fl oz) sunflower oil

The sunflower seeds may be lightly roasted, if desired (see page 182 'Nut Butter' recipe for details of how to do this), but this is

not essential. However roasting does improve the flavour.
Grind the sunflower seeds in a liquidiser or blender until fairly
fine. Gradually add the oil by pouring through the porthole in the
lid while the machine is running, until the oil is all incorporated
and the mixture is smooth. Season to taste and store in a screw-
topped jar in the refrigerator.

C E Gl Gr Pumpkin Seed Spread

Use recipe and method for 'Sunflower Seed Spread' substituting
pumpkin seeds and pumpkin seed oil for sunflower.

C E Gl Gr Safflower Seed Spread

Use recipe and method for 'Sunflower Seed Spread' substituting
safflower seeds and safflower oil for sunflower.

□ E Gl Gr Apricot Egg Replacer

175g (6 oz) unsulphured   *350ml (12 fl oz) water*
  dried apricots

Put the water and washed apricots into a saucepan and boil until
the apricots are soft. Leave to cool, then blend in a blender or
food processor. Store in the refrigerator. 30ml (2 tbsp) is equivalent
to 1 egg.

□ E Gl Gr Date Egg Replacer

Follow recipe and method for 'Apricot Egg Replacer' substituting
dates for apricots.

The above two egg replacers are suitable for binding and bulking
in waffles, pancakes, drop scones and heavier cakes. They are
not suitable where aeration is required.

Drinks

Lemonade

2 large or 3 small lemons
900g (2 lb) sugar or 575g
(1¼ lb) fructose

Up to 15g (½ oz) citric acid
850ml (1½ pt) boiling water

Wash fruit thoroughly. Squeeze out juice and put into a mixing bowl. Remove pith and put peel through mincer. Add the sugar or fructose and mix together. Pour on boiling water, stir to dissolve sugar or fructose and leave overnight (covered). Next day add the citric acid, a little at a time, checking between each addition until the flavour is right. Put through a strainer or muslin bag and bottle. Keep in refrigerator and dilute to taste as required.

Blackberry Syrup

Stew the blackberries with 150ml (¼ pt) water to every 1·350 kg (3 lb) fruit, until all the juice is drawn. Strain, and for every ½ litre (1 pt) juice add 175g (6 oz) sugar. Boil for 15 minutes and bottle for use when cold. Serve diluted to taste with hot or cold water.

As this syrup contains no preservatives, store the bottles in the refrigerator. It makes a pleasant drink for cold winter evenings when diluted with hot water.

Lemon Barley Water

75g (3 oz) pearl barley   *25–40g (1–1½ oz) sugar or*
1 medium-sized lemon   *15–20g (½-¾ oz) fructose*

Put the pearl barley into a saucepan and cover with cold water. Boil for 5 minutes. Drain. Add 1 litre (2 pt) cold water and bring back to boil. Cover and simmer for 30 minutes. Wash and thinly peel the lemon zest. Add to saucepan and continue to simmer for a further 30 minutes. Squeeze out juice from lemon and strain. Put aside. Strain liquid in saucepan into a bowl or jug and add sweetener to taste. When cold stir in lemon juice.

Bottle and store in the refrigerator. Keeps up to 1 week.

Blackcurrant Barley Water

Barley Water is traditionally made with pearl barley but is equally good and much quicker to make using barley flakes.

225g (8 oz) blackcurrants   *50g (2 oz) barley flakes*
1·7 litres (3 pt) water   *Sweetener to taste*

Stew the blackcurrants in the water until the juice is extracted. Add the barley flakes and continue to cook until the mixture thickens. Line a bowl with muslin and strain out all the juice. Serve hot or cold, diluted if you prefer, and sweeten to taste. This drink is good for coughs and colds, so keep some blackcurrants in the freezer in readiness for the winter.

⊞ Ginger Beer

450g (1 lb) demerara sugar   *15g (½ oz) cream of tartar*
1 lemon, sliced   *4·5 litres (1 gallon) water*
50g (2 oz) root ginger   *15g (½ oz) dried yeast*

Boil the water. Put sugar, sliced lemon, ginger and cream of tartar into a large container and pour the boiling water over them. Allow to cool to lukewarm, then add the yeast and leave for 24 hours in a warm place. Strain through muslin and pour into strong bottles with screw tops. Store for 3–4 days when the ginger beer will be ready to drink.

Sweets

 ## Coconut Ice

450g (1 lb) granulated sugar
150ml (¼ pt) goats' milk
  or sheep's milk

150g (5 oz) unsulphured
  desiccated coconut
Natural red colouring
  (optional)

Brush a 18cm (7") square tin with oil or melted milk-free margarine. Place sugar and milk in a very heavy-based saucepan. Stir over a low heat until sugar has dissolved. Bring to boil and boil quickly, without stirring, for about 10 minutes, until 'soft-ball' stage is reached (116°C, 240°F on a sugar thermometer), or until a little, when dropped in a saucer of cold water, just forms a soft ball. Remove saucepan from heat, add coconut and stir until mixture begins to thicken. Pour half the mixture into prepared tin. Put 15ml (1 tbsp) of the remainder into a cup, add a little natural red food colouring and mix well. Add the coloured mixture to the remainder left in the pan and mix well. Pour coloured mixture over that already in the tin. Leave until almost set; mark into 10 bars. When cold, turn out of tin and cut into bars.

Honeycomb

225g (8 oz) sugar
Small pinch of cream of
  tartar
60ml (4 tbsp) cold water

15ml (1 tbsp) golden syrup
1·25ml (¼ tsp) bicarbonate
  of soda
A little warm water

Put the sugar, cream of tartar, syrup and cold water into a large
strong pan. Stir over low heat until sugar has dissolved. Boil
without stirring to 154°C, 310°F on a sugar thermometer. Remove
from heat. Mix the bicarbonate of soda with a little warm water
and add to the boiling hot toffee. (It will froth right up, hence the
need for a large pan). Stir gently and pour into a greased or oiled
tin.

Turkish Delight

450g (1 lb) granulated sugar
1·25ml (¼ tsp) cream of tartar
100g (3½ oz) cornflour
215g (7½ oz) icing sugar
575ml (1 pt) cold water

50g (2 oz) clear honey
10ml (2 tsp) distilled
  rose water
Natural red colouring
  (optional)

Lightly grease or oil a shallow 18cm (7") square tin. Place
granulated sugar and 150ml (¼ pt) water in a heavy-based
saucepan. Stir over a moderate heat until sugar has dissolved.
Bring to boil and boil quickly, without stirring, until 'soft-ball'
stage is reached (116°C, 240°F on a sugar thermometer), or until
a little, when dropped in a saucer of cold water, will just form a
soft ball. Remove from heat, stir in cream of tartar and then leave
on one side. While syrup is cooling, mix 75g (3 oz) cornflour and
200g (7 oz) icing sugar in a large saucepan with a little cold
water, taken from the measured 575ml (1 pt). Add remaining
water. Bring to the boil, stirring all the time and cook for 2 minutes.
Reduce heat and gradually pour the cooled syrup into the cornflour
mixture, beating well with a wooden spoon. Bring to the boil and
boil for 20–30 minutes over a low heat, stirring continuously,
when mixture should be very pale straw in colour and transparent.
Add honey and rose water. Mix thoroughly. Pour half the mixture
into prepared tin. Put 15ml (1 tbsp) of the remainder into a cup,
add a little natural red food colouring and mix well. Add the

coloured mixture to the remainder left in the pan and mix well. Pour over the mixture already in the tin. Leave until quite cold. Dip a sharp knife into icing sugar and cut Turkish Delight into 2·5cm (1") bars. Mix the remaining 15g (½ oz) cornflour and 15g (½ oz) icing sugar together and roll bars in mixture to coat evenly. Leave for 3–4 hours, then cut into 2·5cm (1") squares and coat again in the cornflour and sugar mixture. Leave overnight. Pack. Makes 49 pieces.

Nut Brittle

50–115g (2–4 oz) nuts of choice   5ml (1 tsp) lemon juice
115g (4 oz) icing sugar

Blanch, roast and chop the nuts. Sieve sugar if lumpy, and place with lemon juice into a pan over gentle heat. Heat until golden brown. DO NOT BEAT but stir very gently with a wooden spoon until evenly browned. Stir in finely chopped nuts. Pour into a greased or oiled tin. Mark while warm into squares. Break when cold and store in an airtight jar.

Honey and Treacle Toffee

60ml (4 tbsp) water   15ml (1 tbsp) black treacle
115g (4 oz) milk-free   500g (1 lb 2 oz) muscovado
  margarine   sugar
30ml (2 tbsp) clear honey

Place all the ingredients in a heavy-based saucepan. Heat slowly, stirring until sugar dissolves and margarine melts. Bring to the boil, then cover pan and boil gently for 2 minutes. Uncover and continue to boil, stirring occasionally, for 10–15 minutes (or until a little of the mixture, dropped into a cup of cold water, separates into hard and brittle threads). Pour into greased 15cm (6") square tin and leave until hard, then break with a small hammer. Store in a screw-topped jar.

Treacle Bites

25g (1 oz) barley flour, millet
flour or buckwheat flour
2·5ml (½ tsp) gluten-free
baking powder
Pinch of salt
25g (1 oz) milk-free
margarine
45ml (3 tbsp) black treacle

135g (4½ oz) millet flakes,
buckwheat flakes or
porridge oats
25g (1 oz) demerara sugar
1 egg, beaten
A few drops of Bourbon
vanilla extract
A little grated lemon rind

Sieve flour, baking powder and salt together. Melt milk-free margarine in a saucepan together with the black treacle. Add all the rest of the ingredients and mix well. Drop from a teaspoon in rounds 4cm (1½") apart onto a greased baking sheet. Bake at 190ºC, 375ºF, Gas Mark 5 for 10–15 minutes. Makes 12.

Gl Use millet flakes and millet flour or buckwheat flakes and buckwheat flour.
Gr Use buckwheat flakes or buckwheat flour.

Fruit and Nut Bars

75g (3 oz) natural raisins
or natural sultanas
40g (1½ oz) figs or dates
40g (1½ oz) nuts or grated
fresh coconut
1 eating apple or banana

15ml (1 tbsp) fruit juice
Approx. 50g (2 oz)
powdered goats' milk,
powdered sheep's milk
or powdered soya milk
1 sheet of rice paper

Put first four ingredients through a mincer into a bowl. Add juice and mix thoroughly. Add powdered goats' milk, powdered sheep's milk or powdered soya milk and mix to a firm dry paste. Turn onto a sheet of rice paper and press down firmly to 1·25cm (½") thickness or less. Chill. Cut into bars.

Rum Truffles

90ml (6 tbsp) maple syrup
  or honey
90ml (6 tbsp) 'Meridian
  Hazelnut Butter' or
  'Hazelnut Butter'
  (see page 187)
20g (¾ oz) powdered goats'
  milk, powdered sheep's milk
  or powdered soya milk
10ml (2 tsp) rum

50g (2 oz) porridge oats,
  buckwheat flakes or
  millet flakes
40g (1½ oz) hazelnuts,
  finely chopped
45ml (3 tbsp) cocoa powder
  or carob powder
5ml (1 tsp) lemon rind,
  finely grated

Mix all ingredients together. Form into small balls, and roll them in extra cocoa powder or carob powder. Put into paper sweet cases.

Gl Use millet flakes or buckwheat flakes.
Gr Use buckwheat flakes.

 ## Chocolate or Carob Candies

100g (3½ oz) 'Green and
  Black's Organic Dark
  Chocolate' or 'Plamil
  Carob Confection'
15ml (1 tbsp) black treacle

15ml (1 tbsp) honey
50g (2 oz) porridge oats,
  buckwheat flakes or
  millet flakes
50g (2 oz) natural raisins,
  chopped

Melt the chocolate or carob with the treacle and honey in a bowl over a saucepan of hot water. Mix in the flakes and raisins. Spoon into sweet cases. Makes 20.

Gl Use buckwheat flakes or millet flakes.
Gr Use buckwheat flakes.

Plant Food Families

LATIN	ENGLISH	
Aceraceae	Acer	Maple
Actinidiaceae	Kiwi	Kiwi fruit (Chinese gooseberry)
Alliaceae	Onion	Onion, garlic, chives, leeks, spring onions, scallions, shallots, Chinese chives
Amaranthaceae	Amaranth	Amaranth
Anacardiaceae	Cashew	Pistachio, mango, cashew
Ananas	Pineapple	Pineapple
Anonaceae	Sop	Sour sop, sweet sop, cherimoya
Aquifoliaceae	Holly	Maté tea
Araceae	Arum	Taro, eddo, dasheen, tannia, ceriman, St. Vincent arrowroot
Asparagaceae	Asparagus	Asparagus
Boraginaceae	Borage	Comfrey, borage
Cannabiaceae	Hemp	Hop
Capparidaceae	Caper	Caper
Caprifoliaceae	Honeysuckle	Elderberry
Caricaceae	Papaya	Pawpaw, papaya
Caryophyllaceae	Pink	Claytonia (winter purslane), chickweed
Chenopodiaceae	Goosefoot	Spinach, sugarbeet, beetroot, swiss chard, orache, Good King Henry
Compositae	Daisy	Chicory, dandelion, tarragon, lettuce, alecost, sunflower, cardoon, wormwood, chamomile, Jerusalem artichoke, endive, globe artichoke, sesame, safflower, chinese leaves, salsify, scorzonera, feverfew, tansy, radicchio rosso, pot marigold
Convolvulaceae	Bindweed	Sweet potato
Corylaceae	Birch	Filberts, hazelnuts, cobnuts
Cruciferae	Wallflower	Mustard, radish, turnip, horseradish, cabbage, watercress, broccoli, calabrese, cress, cauliflower, kale, kohlrabi, brussel sprouts, swede (rutabaga), seakale, rocket, rapeseed, chinese greens (pak-choi, pe-tsai, wong bok and shungiku)
Cucurbitaceae	Gourd	Cucumber, pumpkin, melon, courgette, watermelon, squash, gherkin, marrow, chayote, gourd, zucchini
Cupressaceae	Cypress	Juniper berries

Cyperaceae	Sedge	Chinese water chestnut
Dioscorea	Yam	Yam, chinese yam (chinese potato)
Diospyros	Ebony	Persimmon
Ericaceae	Erica	Arbutus (strawberry tree), cranberry, blueberry (bilberry), cowberry, whortleberry
Euphorbiaceae	Spurge	Tapioca (manioc, cassava)
Fagaceae	Beech	Sweet chestnut
Fungi	Fungi	Mushroom, yeast, truffle
Graminae	Grass	Wheat, corn (maize, sweet corn), rice, oats, barley, rye, cane, millet, bamboo, sorghum, wild rice, red rice, lemon grass
Grossulariaceae	Gooseberry	Gooseberry, blackcurrant, red currant, white currant
Iridaceae	Iris	Saffron
Juglans	Walnut	Butternut, hickory nut, walnut, pecan
Labiatae	Mint	Peppermint, spearmint, thyme, marjoram, basil, oregano, bush basil, summer savory, winter savory, sage, rosemary, lemon balm, bergamot, hyssop, lemon thyme, pot marjoram
Lauraceae	Laurel	Avocado, cinnamon, bay leaf
Leguminosae or *Papilionaceae*	Legume or Pea	Pea, all varieties of dried beans, soya, lima beans, lentils, peanuts, groundnuts, liquorice, carob, gram, mung beans, alfalfa, chick pea (garbanzo bean), broad bean, runner bean, fenugreek, tamarind, French bean, yam bean, Morton Bay chestnut
Linaceae	Flax	Linseed (flax)
Malvaceae	Mallow	Okra pods, cotton seed, hibiscus flowers
Moraceae	Mulberry	Fig, mulberry, breadfruit, jackfruit
Musaceae	Banana	Banana, arrowroot, plantain
Myristica	Nutmeg	Nutmeg, mace
Myrtaceae	Myrtle	Allspice, pimento, cloves, guava
Nymphaeaceae	Water Lily	Lotus
Oleaceae	Olive	Olive
Onagraceae	Willow-herb	Water chestnut, singhara nut
Orchidaceae	Orchid	Vanilla
Palmae	Palm	Coconut, date, sago, palm oil, date palm sugar
Papaveraceae	Poppy	Poppy seed
Passiflora	Passionflower	Passion fruit, giant granadilla
Pinaceae	Pine	Pine nuts
Piperaceae	Peppercorns	Black and white peppercorns

Polygonaceae	Knotweed	Buckwheat, rhubarb, sorrel
Proteacea	Macadamia	Macadamia or Queensland nut
Punicaceae	Pomegranate	Pomegranate
Rosaceae	Rose	Apple, pear, quince, japonica quince, medlar, loquat, crab-apple, rowan, azarole, rosehip, strawberry, salad burnet, service tree (sorbitol) *Subgenus Prunus:* plum, peach, cherry, apricot, almond, nectarine, sloe, damson, bullace, greengage *Subgenus Rubus:* raspberry, cloudberry, loganberry, blackberry, wineberry, dewberry, boysenberry
Rubiaceae	Madder	Coffee
Rutaceae	Citrus	Lemon, grapefruit, tangerine, orange, satsuma, lime, citron, kumquat, ugli fruit, clementine
Sapindaceae	Lychee	Rambutan, lychee
Solanaceae	Potato	Tomato, potato, eggplant (aubergine), chilli, sweet pepper (capsicum), cayenne, ground cherries, tomatillo (jamberry), cape gooseberry, huckleberry, paprika
Subcaya	Brazil Nut	Brazil nut
Theaceae	Camellia	Tea
Theobroma	Cocoa	Cocoa
Tiliaceae	Lime	Linden flowers
Umbelliferae	Hemlock	Carrot, parsnip, celery, anise, parsley, caraway, celeriac, dill, coriander, fennel, cumin, chervil, lovage, angelica, samphire, sweet cicely
Urticaceae	Nettle	Nettle
Valerianaceae	Valerian	Lamb's lettuce (corn salad)
Vitaceae	Vine	Grape, raisin, sultana, currant
Zingiberaceae	Ginger	Ginger, turmeric, curcumin

Index

M